SUCCESSFUL BUSINESS PRESENTATIONS

MANAGEMENT SKILL GUIDE

SUCCESSFUL BUSINESS PRESENTATIONS

Howell Parry

Croner Publications Limited
Croner House
London Road
Kingston upon Thames
Surrey KT2 6SR
Telephone: 081–547 3333

First published 1991
Reprinted 1994

Published by
Croner Publications Ltd,
Croner House,
London Road,
Kingston upon Thames,
Surrey KT2 6SR
Telephone: 081–547 3333

While every care has been taken in the writing and editing of this book, readers should be aware that only Acts of Parliament and Statutory Instruments have the force of law, and that only the courts can authoritatively interpret the law.

British Library Cataloguing-in-Publication Data
Parry, Howell
Successful business presentations.
I. Title
808.5

ISBN 1–885524–051–3

Phototypeset by Intype, London
Printed by Watkiss Studios Ltd., Biggleswade, Bedfordshire

Contents

Introduction

The ability to make a decent presentation is a precious business tool, without which managers, executives or professionals in industry, commerce or administration are incompletely equipped to do their jobs. People in this group — who may be described broadly as business people — cannot avoid making presentations, at least occasionally. Their jobs require them to inform or persuade, sometimes exhort, audiences made up of colleagues, customers, suppliers, officials or fellow professionals. These may be formal or informal occasions and audiences may vary in size, but all have the common feature that both presenter and audience are there as part of the job.

For many people, unfortunately, making even a simple presentation can be at best a worry and at worst an ordeal, and business people are no exception. Uneasiness apart, however, comparatively few in positions of responsibility in business are good presenters. Some make a brave attempt and usually improve with practice and experience. But too many appear to take their indifferent performance for granted and tend to avoid presentations as far as possible.

Why Make a Presentation?

In business, as in other walks of life, it is necessary to communicate. Notes, plans, specifications, reports and sets of accounts are circulated, and day in and day out business people have to talk to each other. But, if many people are involved in the same affair, individual exchanges can take too long and it is more convenient to get the group together and address them collectively. A written message may, in theory, serve the purpose equally well, but more often than not the spoken word makes a stronger impact than the written.

The first reason for this is that, if there is an alternative, many people avoid reading. The popularity of dramatised versions of books is an immediate example of the common preference for the spoken word (if possible with illustrations) over the written. The writer and actors portray the characters and background; the audience are given the story with the "boring" bits cut out.

So it is with the spoken word in business. A presenter summarises, selects and emphasises the important matters and sorts the wheat from the chaff.

Secondly, when people are face to face they can make a judgement about each other in a way that is not possible through the written word. The impression those in an audience gain of the presenter provides a basis (not, of course, the only basis) for their assessment of the communication.

Thirdly, the members of an audience are able to observe and relate to the reaction of others. Reading tends to be a solitary activity, in which impressions are relatively unaffected by those of other readers. This may be intellectually beneficial, but it is undoubtedly useful and reassuring to have an idea of the strength of other views.

A fourth advantage of presentations is that they provide an opportunity for give and take. Through questions and discussion, presenter and audience can fill the gaps, tie up loose ends and resolve doubts.

What Needs to be Done?

Why then, if the ability to make a presentation is so important, is the standard among business people so disappointing and what can be done about it?

There is a commonly held idea that presentations are something people are good at or not and that it does more harm than good to attempt something of which they are likely to make a hash. There is even a tendency in some quarters to beware of those who have too glib a tongue, and there still seem to be a few diehards who regard themselves as "plain people" whose position requires them to make an occasional presentation and believe that when this unfortunately happens it is up to the audience to make the best of what is offered.

Negative attitudes of this kind are misplaced. With knowledge of what to do, it is perfectly possible, without necessarily having a natural flair, to approach presentations positively and perform them successfully.

This guide does two things. It provides a logical, step-by-step procedure, covering the essential aspects of business presentations. It also discusses the principles on which successful communication between presenter and audience is based.

Not that there is a magic formula: on the contrary, the guide's prescription, although easily understood, calls for considerable personal effort, but effort which can lead to steady improvement and growth of satisfaction. The aim throughout is to break down the barriers, often self-erected, that face budding presenters.

And while the emphasis is on business presentations and the illustrations are related to business circumstances, the principles are universal and can be applied equally to any situation where a person is attempting to convey a message by word of mouth to others.

The Structure of the Guide

Successful presentation is based on knowledge of the subject, sound preparation and competent delivery.

Since business presenters will, by definition, be talking about their job, the first of these should present few difficulties, although an important part of preparation is to assemble the facts and repair any gaps encountered. But the main concern is less with the raw material than with getting it to the audience and the guide is therefore set out under the two broad divisions of preparation and delivery.

Priority of place, however, is given to a chapter about nerves, which can affect able and experienced presenters as well as beginners. The former have learned from experience, however, that it is possible to make a good job of presentation and actually enjoy doing it despite nerves. But, since nerves can be a strong enough deterrent to prevent many people from even attempting a presentation, the subject is tackled before anything else.

There follows the main chapter on preparation, which deals with the translation of the raw material into words, and there are separate chapters on choice of language, the working script and visual aids. The last three items are essential components of preparation, but sufficiently distinct to stand alone.

Then comes a chapter on delivery, supplemented by one on good and bad habits connected with humour, audibility, gesture and movement, and mannerisms. The important subject of handling questions also has a chapter of its own.

The final chapter deals with rehearsal, which incorporates some suggestions on the related subject of general practice. Rehearsal is, of course, logically part of preparation, but it cannot be discussed properly without first understanding how a presentation should be delivered.

One further word about practice is needed. Understanding the theory is one thing: but reliable results are unlikely without practice; and the best form of practice is actually making presentations to an audience, so that presenters can learn from their mistakes and gain satisfaction and increasing confidence from their successes.

Chapter 1
Nerves

An honest discussion about making a presentation has to face squarely the question of nerves. It would be convenient to dismiss nerves as no more than an incidental nuisance and comforting to supply a reliable remedy. Neither is possible. The majority of beginners, and many who have been at it a long time, worry about the prospect of making a presentation. Experience confirms, however, that nerves, if not eradicable, are conquerable.

The impact of nerves can vary from extreme worry to an exhilarating sense of anticipation. It is a mistake to think that those who obviously enjoy and are good at presentation are without nerves. Some of the best admit to butterflies in the stomach, and worse, before the event. Furthermore, many professional public performers with established reputations are harassed by nerves every time they appear, difficult as it may be for a novice to believe this.

Psychologists tell us that nerves are more accurately described as anxiety and it is true that there are quite a number of things presenters might properly be anxious about. Much may hang on the success of their presentation; their prestige and prospects may be on the line; there are potential hazards, like misjudgement of the audience's expectations, that they do their best to anticipate, but cannot absolutely predict; or something may go wrong with the mechanics. One example was a power cut that occurred during a presentation which relied heavily on the overhead projector.

Adverse circumstances like these do not occur often, but most presenters remain conscious of the risk and some refuse to listen to their common sense, which tells them the risk is remote.

But, hazards apart, those who embark on a presentation simply want to do well; they want the audience to be pleased with them, and the fear, however ill-founded, that they may not do themselves justice is enough to make them tense.

Suffering from nerves should not be confused with lack of confidence. It is possible to be confident but still nervous. On the other hand, soundly based confidence is the means by which nerves are surmounted. A measure of confidence is acquired through experience, but this is not enough in itself and needs to be reinforced by means of careful preparation, which is the primary source of confidence. Presenters who are well prepared find that nerves, even if still lurking in the background, are no impediment once they get under way. They gain reassurance from discovering consistently that nerves do not prevent them from performing well; that nerves are a surmountable obstacle.

Experienced presenters know, and beginners come to learn, that the way to handle nerves is to press on regardless, so that their preparation and underlying confidence can assert themselves. They find that their best armour is to expect nerves while remaining confident that they can cope. It follows, of course, that the more presentations they make, the greater will be their confidence in their ability to cope.

Psychologists also make the point, however, that anxiety is actually helpful to presenters. They explain that for any given activity there is an optimum level of arousal (as they call the physiological state associated with anxiety), which in the case of a presentation is fairly high and has the benefit of focusing attention and encouraging alertness and the ability to think quickly. In short, it might be said in lay terminology that nerves keep presenters on their toes.

Nerves have another positive aspect in that they discourage presenters from taking their audience for granted. There are a minority of presenters who appear to have complete assurance, but who seem too often to regard the audience as almost an irrelevance. Nerves may be Nature's way of reminding presenters that their first duty is to the audience.

Good presenters anticipate the hazards ahead, are aware of the essential unpredictability of those they hope will be listening to them and are mindful of the element of risk in what they are doing. They are, in short, nervous, but from this they derive a sense of excitement which makes a successfully executed presentation very satisfying.

So far, nerves have been considered in their rational and controllable sense. There are, however, a few who suffer to an *irrational* extent. They may know they are well prepared; they may even know from experience that they usually make a good presentation; they may expect a friendly audience — but still they do not believe it when the time comes. Presentations are to them an almost intolerable trial. It would be a pity if they were deprived thereby of the benefit of a business tool of great usefulness, which in some jobs would be indispensable.

Fortunately there is a method of self-help which many have found useful. It goes like this. Presenters should ask themselves:

(a) What is the worst thing that could happen?
(b) How likely is it to happen?
(c) If it did happen, how bad would it really be and what could be done about it?

Objective answers to these questions can help to get things into perspective, so that presenters stop worrying unduly about the improbable and find that even the unthinkable is manageable.

There is also a useful relaxation exercise based on breathing, as follows.

(a) Sit back in an armchair, or lie on a bed, with eyes closed.
(b) Breathe from the diaphragm (the abdomen should bulge outwards, on breathing in).
(c) Slow down the rate of breathing, aiming initially at three seconds to breathe in and four seconds to breathe out, but slower if comfortable. Put the emphasis on exhaling, making it last a second or two longer than inhaling.

This should be practised at least once a day for a few weeks, so that it can be used proficiently, if the need arises, before a presentation. (Users of the technique have to make themselves as comfortable as possible in the likely absence of an armchair or bed.) This technique is not designed to provide complete relaxation — which would not be a good idea at such a time — but merely enough to induce an optimum level of attention and alertness.

Ian Woosnam, the golfer, on winning the Suntory World Match Play Championship, admitted that he still got nervous "especially in events like this one, but I've learned the value of deep breathing to relax before hitting shots".

Very few people suffer from nerves to the point where they absolutely cannot go on. Thorough preparation is the most reliable insurance against such a predicament. Most business people are capable, with experience, and always provided they are well prepared, of doing justice to a presentation despite nerves. True, it is necessary to persevere, but the reward is that nerves become no longer a hindrance; on the contrary, they give an edge that would otherwise be lacking. It might even be said that presenters who do not suffer from nerves at all really have something to worry about.

Summary

(a) Most normal people suffer from nerves when they make a presentation because they are aware that snags can arise.
(b) Confidence, based on experience and adequate preparation, enables them to surmount nerves.
(c) If they press on despite nerves they find their nerves recede and are no impediment to a successful performance.
(d) On the positive side, nerves, under control, actually sharpen their performance and also prevent them from taking the audience for granted.
(e) Some simple psychological exercises are available which can help those who suffer seriously from nerves.

Chapter 2
Preparation

A Drill for Preparation

It is not impossible to make a good presentation without the benefit of preparation. A few accomplished presenters, who have a clear mind, deliberate temperament and thorough knowledge of their subject, may be able to do it, although it is certain they would do it even better had they the opportunity to prepare.

But for most people effective preparation is an essential foundation for successful presentation. The better prepared they are, the better their performance will be, the less they will be bothered by nerves, the easier it will be to get on terms with the audience, and the more economical use they will make of the time available.

What can they do, however, if they are genuinely caught "on the hop" — if, for example, they are called upon unexpectedly to explain a process to a group of visitors? The answer is to do as much preparation as possible. It is not really good enough to leave things to chance and rely on professional knowledge and native wit. In practice there is always time to do *some* preparation and the best use should be made of whatever limited time is available.

One thing that can be done is anticipate the *possibility* of making a presentation. While this may not always be practicable, it can often be predicted that a call to make a presentation is likely. There is gain all round if, as a result of some preparation, the performance is more effective than might be expected in the circumstances.

This chapter suggests a logical system for preparing a presentation. The aim should be, of course, to start preparation as far in advance as possible. However, if the time available is genuinely restricted it is a great help to have a drill available, which — with practice — comes automatically, enabling any presentation to be approached with enhanced confidence.

Repeat Performances

An old hand was once lecturing a group of novices. He began: "I haven't prepared anything special; I'll just ramble on and let you ask questions". And ramble on he did, obviously using the framework of a talk he had been giving for years. There was no logical form, no bite; more a series of apparently much-used anecdotes. As for questions, it was difficult to get a word in edgeways.

It is easy to become complacent about repeat performances, especially if they have gone down well on a previous occasion. Presenters should, therefore, make it a rule to review the text each time and see whether changes can usefully be made. Doing this, and also adjusting the approach (if necessary) will do much to keep a presentation sharp and fresh.

The ideal is for those on the receiving end to feel that the presentation has been designed especially for them (a point to be developed later), but this is difficult when relying on an old text which has not been regularly updated.

Joint Presentations

The need for coordination in joint presentations may seem obvious, but all too often there is overlap and sometimes mutual contradiction. Coordination may not be easy, especially if the contributors are at different locations; in addition, some presenters are prone to guard their material jealousy. Without coordination in joint presentations, however, there is a high risk of a foul up.

Preparing the Text

Whether reading a presentation, committing it to memory or using notes (options that will be considered in due course), it is necessary to start from a basic text, using the words, phrases and framework that will best convey the presenter's ideas.

Before putting anything on paper presenters need a focus. They must consider their aim: what is it that they are hoping to achieve in making a presentation on this particular theme, on this particular occasion, to this particular audience? The aim may be, for example, to impart information; to persuade others to a point of view; to deflect criticism; to gain support; or to make a report — all these are typical and familiar reasons for a business presentation. This question — why? — is a vital starting point on which may depend the answers to a number of other questions that will be considered presently, especially if there is a conflict of priorities.

One important point should be borne in mind before preparing for a presentation: never overload the audience with more than they can absorb.

> One of the most famous politicians of the post-war years was told after his maiden speech in the House of Commons that he had tried to make too many points. The elder statesman who advised him suggested that a back-bencher should never make more than one point in a speech; a minister, two; and a Prime Minister, possibly three, but better still two. The art of speaking, he was told, was to convey a clear picture to the audience, not write an essay about it.

This principle is as valid in business as in politics, perhaps more so. Adding a secondary theme merely dilutes the impact of the main message and may so confuse the audience that no impact is made at all.

And if, in exceptional circumstances, there is no choice but to deal with more than one theme, make sure they are clearly distinguishable and not mutually confusing.

The Material for the Text

The foundation of any business presentation is knowledge of the subject. As most people will be dealing with a subject connected with their own job, they will either have the necessary information or know where to find it. It is essential never to set out to make a business presentation without true knowledge of the subject. All the eloquence in the world will not conceal ignorance: a high proportion of the audience may be as well informed as the presenter!

A good start is to put on paper all the information and ideas to be imparted. It is not necessary at this stage to worry about how the material is to be assembled for delivery. It should be set out in the order it comes to mind and the empty spaces can be filled in due course. The next stage is to arrange the material under sub-headings, a process that will impose a systematic framework and indicate any gaps in the presenter's knowledge or weaknesses in reasoning.

A great deal of work can be saved by abstracting some or all of the material needed from existing files, notes or other sources, but it will not necessarily be in a form suitable for a presentation. It may need rearrangement.

What? Who? How Long?

The next stage is to assemble the basic material in a form that will make the most effective impact. Three questions have to be answered:

(a) What? (What is the message to be conveyed?)
(b) Who? (What are the characteristics of the audience?)
(c) How long? (How long should the presentation last?)

Experienced presenters find that these questions occur to them spontaneously. Very often the answers will be obvious, but sometimes they need a bit of thought and research. If there is little time to prepare, it is necessary to determine the answers as accurately as possible in the time available, but failure to address these questions will cause the effectiveness of the presentation to suffer.

The material should be divided into three groups:

(a) the essential,
(b) the non-essential (this does not mean the unimportant) and
(c) the anecdotal.

It is necessary to be selective in deciding what is essential, in order not to debase the currency and because there is a limit to the number of ideas an audience can assimilate. It is essential that the audience understand and retain the essential points.

Non-essential material can be held in reserve and may be included if there is time; its omission, however, should not be detrimental to the main thrust of the presentation.

The third category of material is the anecdotal: instances and examples which illuminate facts and opinions. The purpose of anecdotal material is to divert, provide practical illustrations and introduce a human note. Audiences, almost without exception, relate positively to a brief, topical and appropriate anecdote. A reminiscence about something that has gone wrong often has a particularly striking effect. Visual aids serve a similar illustrative purpose.

A chemist was describing a new method of analysis she had developed, which was an improvement on her previous technique. She avoided excessive technical detail and described how there was formerly a danger, if the analyst missed the critical point, of ending up with a useless gluey deposit. She then produced a retort, its bottom solid with a yellow gum. Her audience immediately identified with the mishap and enjoyed this highly effective combination of anecdote and visual aid.

It is sometimes even worth pruning essential material in order to find time for an apposite anecdote and presenters should always try to keep a couple of "spares" up their sleeves, in case of need.

Some of the most effective anecdotes are delivered apparently off the cuff and if they have an edge of humour, so much the better (see Chapter 7).

Who?

It is important not to misjudge the audience. If they come expecting one kind of presentation and something else has been prepared, its reception will suffer, unless the presenter senses the situation in time and makes an adjustment. (Most presenters get into this morass sometimes and some advice is offered later about what can be done about it.) It is obviously better to try to avoid any such difficulty by taking some trouble to define the composition of the audience as accurately as possible.

Here are some of the things to be investigated.

(a) Background	— Are the audience serious minded and committed or likely to respond better to a lighter approach?
(b) Needs	— Is there any particular gap in understanding that has to be filled?
(c) Knowledge	— Are the audience well informed about the subject and, if not, do they have the background knowledge to allow easy comprehension?
(d) Interests	— Have the audience a direct interest in the subject and, if so, is this interest general or related to a particular aspect?
(e) Patient	— What sort of appetite for a presentation are the audience likely to have? Are they used to listening and remaining alert for a reasonable length of time?
(f) Receptiveness	— Are the audience likely to be looking forward to listening to the presentation?
(g) Status	— Are the group senior, junior or equal to the presenter?
(h) Preoccupation	— Are the audience or any significant number of them likely to have anything else in mind that might act as a diversion?

Audience characteristics are a complex matter, which it is worth taking trouble to analyse and make some enquiries about if information is limited. The composition of the audience is of considerable importance in determining "what?" (the essential, the non-essential and the anecdotal) and has also to be taken into account in considering the time element.

Another question related to "who?" is "how many?". This has a bearing on other aspects of preparation, such as seating, visual aids and the way questions are handled. Many presenters have come unstuck because they arrived expecting a large audience and found a handful and *vice versa*.

How Long?

There is an invariable general rule concerning the length of a presentation: to take less time than expected is acceptable; to take more is not. Many an excellent presentation has lost its impact because the presenter miscalculated the time, failed to watch the clock or thought things were going so well that the audience could take a bit more. The administrative inconveniences of overrunning are plain.

The length of time the presentation takes depends on several factors, some out of the presenter's control.

The first consideration is how long presenters think they need to say their piece, which then has to be related to the amount of time offered. If there is an absolute limit on the latter, it is necessary to do some pruning.

The next question is the prospective audience's stamina: some can take more than others. The presenter's own stamina also has to be considered. In the case of one who is inexperienced and unsure, it may be wise to keep the presentation as short as possible. Another factor is that some subjects and methods of presentation are more exhausting than others.

Finally, it is necessary to consider what proportion of the total time should be devoted to questions and make allowance accordingly.

Compromise

The three questions "what?", "who?" and "how long?" are interdependent but often conflicting. What is essential for one audience may be non-essential for another. The number of anecdotes appropriate for one audience may be unnecessary for a more serious-minded group. And the time element may seriously restrict flexibility.

It is quite often necessary to compromise between "what?", "who?" and "how long?" and the arbitrator between these three is the original question, "why?" — in other words, "What is the aim of making a presentation on this particular theme, on this particular occasion, to this particular audience?"

Getting the Text into Shape

Assembling the basic material and answering the questions "what?" "why?" and "how long?" are relatively uncomplicated tasks. This is not to say they are easy, for they may call for considerable sifting and research, but they require slogging rather than originality, painstaking effort rather than creative imagination.

Creative imagination is, on the other hand, precisely the quality needed to get the text into a shape acceptable to the audience; in a form they will be able to assimilate and understand, and also find interesting and, in appropriate places, arresting.

Here are some guidelines for preparing the narrative.

(a) Make each point in logical order.
(b) Take the audience along in easy stages and make it clear when one stage has ended and another one starts.
(c) Make an interim summing-up from time to time, to help the audience keep pace with the flow.
(d) Repeat important points, but with variations, in order to avoid sounding repetitious. An illustrative anecdote can be helpful in this.
(e) Build up to occasional highlights to draw attention to important bits and also, if necessary, to wake up a flagging audience. But remember that too many highlights are self-defeating.
(f) Recheck or get more facts if there appear to be gaps in information. This may be tiresome and time-consuming, but important, in order to avoid the risk of getting into difficulties on the day.

The Opening Passage

One of the points to be stressed in Chapter 6, which deals with delivery, is the value of making a strong initial impact on the audience. The foundation for this is laid during preparation with the composition of a pithy, striking opening passage, which prepares the audience for what is going to be said (and which must be learnt by heart).

A factory doctor who gave occasional talks on health opened one of his presentations as follows. "My subject today," he led off, "is of the utmost importance to bodily health — I am going to talk about beer." His audience immediately sat up.

The value of framing a closing passage on similar lines is discussed later in the chapter.

Michael Heseltine has related that Lord Stockton once advised him to write the closing passage of a speech *first* as a means of clarifying the mind about its aim.

This is a sound approach, for, although the wording of both opening and closing passages may be changed (perhaps several times) later, the act of framing them concentrates the mind in the right direction.

The Three Step Rule

It is said that all stories should have a beginning, a middle and an end. Asked the secret of his hold over his congregations, a famous evangelist replied: "First I tell them what I am going to say, then I say it, then I tell them what I've said". Again, in music there is the sonata form: namely the exposition, the development and, finally, the recapitulation of a basic theme.

This pattern works, whatever the medium, because it is logical and obvious and appeals to audiences since they can understand what is happening. In a presentation, the formula — called the "three step rule" — becomes the *introduction*, the *development* and the *summing up*.

The three step rule can be used for almost any kind of presentation. The introduction prepares the audience for what is to come; so that its members are more receptive as the theme is developed; and they remember it better it if is summarised at the end. The three step rule is appropriate, not only for the presentation as a whole, but also to clarify any of its stages which is particularly complicated.

Suppose the subject of a presentation is a proposed job evaluation scheme, which is to use a points system. The first step is an introductory statement of intent; the second step a detailed explanation of the proposals; and the third a succinct recapitulation of the proposals. But it may be judged necessary, within the body of the presentation, to say something about the theory of job evaluation, a complex enough subject in itself to require three step rule treatment.

Shaping the Text

Within the three step rule the text can be shaped in whatever manner is most suitable for the purpose.

For example, if the purpose is descriptive or explanatory, presenters should take it in logical sequence. If they are making a commissioned report, the audience should be reminded of the brief, given an explanation of how the task was approached and then a report of the findings. Again, if some recommendation is being made, the background must be explained, the alternatives discussed and the presenter's choice and reasons for it given. For the best effect, the layout has to be adapted according to the purpose; hence the importance of creative imagination. Presenters should not hesitate to seek and listen to suggestions from colleagues, who can be a fruitful source of ideas. In the final analysis, however, presenters must trust their own judgement.

One final point: it is worthwhile being a little adventurous in framing the text. A pedestrian text is in danger of leading to a dull presentation.

Getting the Text on Paper

Many experienced presenters advocate writing out the text of a presentation in full, which is inescapable if it is going to be read out. But, when speaking from notes (as this guide advocates), it is necessary only to summarise each step, although incorporating any particularly vivid turn of phrase or illustration.

Summarising is advantageous for the following reasons:

(a) When every word is set out, it is not always easy to see the wood for the trees. A summary is more flexible, allowing the different parts of the text to be picked out quickly.

(b) A summary is easier to condense into notes, being itself a form of notes, although too voluminous for most presenters.
(c) Recording the text in the form of a summary gets presenters into the habit of thinking in terms of the *gist* of what they wish to say, rather than every last word.

Here is a brief example: assume a speaker is being introduced.

Full text	*Summary*
I am pleased to welcome on your behalf Mr John Smith, whose name is becoming as well known to the general public as it is already to his fellow engineers.	Welcome John Smith. Engineer, becoming generally well known.
We all know that his reputation in the field of hydraulics is second to none.	Reputation in hydraulics second to none.
I am sure you are all looking forward as much as I to hearing him speak.	All looking forward to presentation.
Ladies and gentlemen, John Smith.	Introduce.

Unless presenters are very sure of both subject and audience, and also very experienced, they will undoubtedly feel the need to do a considerable amount of chopping and changing before getting the text into a satisfactory shape. It may seem at times that it will never come right, but, as adjustments are made, parts discarded and sometimes reinstated, they are actually building up, not only the text of the presentation, but also confidence in their ability to deliver it successfully on the day.

As they compose their text, they will be rehearsing in their mind a *version* of what they are going to say. This does not mean that they will be committing their text to memory (apart from their opening and closing sentences). On the contrary, they wish the words they actually use when they make their presentation to appear spontaneous. But, as they prepare — and the more time they give to preparation, the more this will be the case — they will find the "right" words emerging more and more easily. These words and phrases will tend to surface spontaneously during rehearsal and eventually during the presentation.

Timing

Time should be checked as the text is shaped and provisionally noted at intervals, with an allowance for questions; but it should be remembered that presentations tend to take longer in the actual event than is estimated during preparation. Timings will probably have to be revised as preparation proceeds, but presenters should always have a rough idea of how long they expect to take at each stage.

Do not throw away any unused non-essential or anecdotal material. Either may come in handy in reserve.

The Closing Passage

The final stage of getting the text on paper is to decide the form of the last sentence or two (of which, if Lord Stockton's advice has been followed, the presenter will already have at least an idea). As the opening words are intended to prepare the audience by giving it a glimpse of what lies ahead, the closing words should encapsulate the message the presenter wishes to leave. One thing worth mentioning here (although it will be referred to later) is that a few words to follow the question period (if any) should also be drafted: this is an opportunity, therefore, for a final summing up.

Administrative Preparation

Presenters are well advised, as far as possible, to check and, if necessary, adjust the administrative arrangements. Obviously, if the boss says that a presentation is to be made on a certain subject at a certain place at a certain time, and there is no possibility of variation, then "that is that". Among colleagues and outside bodies, however, there is often some flexibility and if it is possible, within reason, to adjust things in a way that makes it substantially easier to perform effectively, presenters should not be afraid to suggest changes.

Reconnaissance of the venue and discussion of the arrangements with the organisers are always advisable; at least get to the venue early enough to have a reasonable look round. Here are some of the things to be borne in mind.

(a) Try to ensure that the size of the room allocated is consistent with the probable size of the audience.
(b) Confirm that the location is reasonably quiet.

A presenter was allocated a corner room of an hotel. The road outside was on a gradient and noisy with heavy lorries. Had this been discovered beforehand something could have been done about it, as the organisers were particularly amenable people, but by the time the presenter got there it was too late.

(c) As for the time of day, personal convenience is more important than whether the audience is likely to be more or less attentive at one time of day than another. The immediacy of a heavy meal or intake of coffee are overrated factors — by far the more potent influence on the attention of the audience is the *quality* of the presentation. On the other hand, the timing of the event in relation to the presenter's other commitments or travelling arrangements can be of significant importance. The presenter should allow as much time as possible to arrive without rushing, to have some refreshment, to check the arrangements and also, after the event, not to feel under too much pressure to leave in a hurry.
(d) Try to ensure that the audience is reasonably concentrated. A dispersed group is difficult to cope with, even by the most proficient presenter, and prevention is easier than cure.

Greville Janner was once giving a paper at the Conference Centre in Harrogate. He had a sizeable audience but it is a large arena and some were scattered in the far corners. He declined to start until they were more compactly seated and the way he marshalled the recalcitrants was a model of tactful determination.

(e) Try to prevent or control interruptions such as a telephone ringing or a secretary coming in with an "urgent" message. Interruptions are sometimes unavoidable, especially if there are senior people present; the best arrangement then is to direct any messages to one person, who can deliver them quietly and unobtrusively. Those arranging presentations do not always think of these things, but will usually do their best to oblige if the matter is raised. (If there is an interruption, treat the disturbance good-humouredly. To make a fuss, which is a sore temptation if things have been going well, does no good and is more likely to spoil the performance than the interruption itself.)

(f) Make sure any equipment is in working order.

Summary

(a) Preparation is the key to a successful presentation and it is always possible to do some, however short the notice.
(b) Try to anticipate the possibility of having to make a presentation.
(c) Refurbish the text as necessary for repeat performances.
(d) Coordinate the preparation of joint presentations.
(e) Base preparation on the question "why?".
(f) Do not overload the audience: one theme is usually enough.
(g) Research the subject thoroughly.
(h) Start by asking "what?", "who?", "how long?"; if there has to be a compromise between them, the deciding factor is "why?".
(i) Divide the material into categories: essential, non-essential and anecdotal. Always make time for some anecdotes.
(j) Compose an arresting opening and closing passage.
(k) Set out the text, in full or in summary, in logical, distinct stages, using the three step formula (introduction, development, summing up) and shaped according to the purpose.
(l) Check the time taken at each step.
(m) Check the administrative arrangements beforehand, if possible on the ground. Make any necessary changes, if practicable and reasonable.

Chapter 3
Language

The ideas in a presenter's mind are expressed in the form of words. It is essential that the listener should understand these words as intended. If the listener's understanding of *words* is defective, his or her perception of *ideas* will also be defective. The listener is then liable either to fill the gaps with substitute and perhaps inaccurate ideas or simply to switch off.

There are, of course, reasons other than the incorrect choice of word or phrase for deficient understanding (expanded on in Chapter 6). The present chapter, however, is concerned not with the way language is *spoken* but with language itself.

The language used is obviously easier to control if the presentation is read (an important reason why it is almost obligatory to read from a prepared text when, as in public announcements, there must be no possibility of misunderstanding). But when speaking from notes, the choice of language has, to some extent, to be extemporaneous; indeed it is a presenter's aim to make it seem so.

With thorough preparation, presenters will of course have a good idea of what they are going to say. But they cannot forecast with certainty what words and phrases will actually emerge at the time. Not that it should be particularly difficult to make the message clear, provided the audience is addressed in simple English, which even in its most basic form is capable of expressing every shade of meaning likely to be needed. Unfortunately, many people are prone to try to embellish and unnecessarily supplement the wonderfully rich language they have at their disposal. The aim of this chapter, therefore, is to suggest a few rules of language which will be of help in avoiding some of its pitfalls.

The words and phrases used should be:

(a) simple
(b) familiar to *all* the audience
(c) unambiguous
(d) tactful and unemotive, and
(e) straight.

Simplicity

It is astonishing how many people, who in the normal way use simple words and phrases, feel it necessary in a presentation (as well as in other "formal" situations) to use more tortuous language.

When the Queen some years ago met a newly appointed US Ambassador and asked him how he was settling into the embassy, he replied (in front of the TV cameras, which perhaps made the situation even more fraught for him) that he was "momentarily engaged in some elements of refurbishment" ("We are making some alterations").

Examples of unnecessary wordiness can be found in virtually every business and profession; civil servants have a particularly notorious, although not always deserved, reputation. The trouble with complicated language is not so much that it is ugly, bad though this is, but that it is liable to be imperfectly understood, misinterpreted or actually unintelligible. There is a further danger: in trying to impress the audience, the presenter may use an obscure expression incorrectly or, on the other hand, the *presenter* may use it correctly but one or more of the audience interpret it incorrectly.

The hazards are obvious, but so are the solutions, which are to:

(a) keep it simple
(b) avoid verbal over indulgence
(c) avoid using a word without being *certain* of its meaning
(d) be self-critical – if in doubt, presenters should ask themselves how *they* would react if they were in the audience and heard the same words.

Familiarity

Specialists tend to use expressions which are commonly and currently in use among their own kind but may be less familiar to outsiders. These expressions include jargon, slang, abbreviations and vogue words. They might be called "insider words", for they are widely used between "insiders", for whom they often (but not always) have a precise meaning and can provide a useful shorthand. To outsiders, however, they may be, at best, only vaguely familiar. It is also unfortunately true that many outsiders *pretend* to understand such words, in order to make it appear that they also are insiders, which clearly increases the risk of misunderstanding.

The rule in presentation is to stick to expressions which are familiar to *all*. This means avoiding (or, if there is no alternative, explaining) insider words, unless it is certain that all the audience know *precisely* what they mean. The main categories of insider words are as follows.

Jargon

This word originally meant "gibberish" or "twittering", but many dictionaries now accept its alternative meaning of "the terminology of a profession". Properly used among people who know what it means, the use of jargon is perfectly acceptable, as it can pithily describe an activity or concept which might otherwise require lengthy definition.

> At the factory of one of our most prestigious clothing manufacturers, sub-standard garments used to be called "pork" and the control dockets that accompanied a garment through the production process were called "jokers" – convenient shorthand for insiders, but incomprehensible to outsiders.

To one who is unfamiliar with its correct usage jargon remains gibberish. Avoid it if there is any possibility of doubt.

Slang

This is a word or phrase in common colloquial use and also suffers from the shortcoming that its precise meaning may not be generally known. But slang often has an attractive raciness and, used sparingly and selectively, it can introduce a welcome light touch, especially if the subject is a bit serious. But it is necessary to avoid any hint of patronising the audience and to be sure that the meaning is understood by all.

Abbreviations

Abbreviations and acronyms are part of everyday life, but are better avoided if there is any chance of confusion. Be particularly wary of TLAs (three letter abbreviations): few audiences would fail to understand BBC (British Broadcasting Corporation) but how many would recognise TQM (total quality management) or JIT (just in time — a production technique)? Again, flu (influenza) or bus (omnibus) have supplanted the longer original forms, but what about "job spec" (job specification)? Expressions that are peculiar to a particular organisation or business are especially risky.

Vogue words

These are expressions which are currently fashionable among "in" people and this guide may indeed, in using the expression, have fallen into its own trap. Are all, or even most, of its readers likely to know what "vogue word" means?

As it happens, this is an appropriate place to point out that sometimes an insider word or phrase which is unfamiliar to the audience may be particularly apt in its context and have no equally pithy equivalent. It is permissible in these exceptional circumstances to use the expression, *provided its meaning is explained beyond any possibility of misunderstanding*.

Many vogue words are an extension of an original, perhaps narrower or slightly different, meaning and often perform a precise and otherwise unfilled role. ("Jargon" used to be one, but is now so familiar that it has ceased to be a vogue word.)

An up-to-date example is "charisma", which originally had a spiritual connotation, but which has come to indicate an aura of personal magnetism, a quality which no other word quite conveys. "Interface" was formerly a mathematical term which has been extended to refer to personal relationships: nothing else seems to match its immediacy. There are other vogue words that have come to play an equally valuable role.

Unfortunately, many vogue words are imprecise, ambiguous, used instead of better existing words, or used in an inappropriate or absurd context. One example is "state of the art".

> Members of a training group were asked what they thought "state of the art" meant. One person suggested "the cultural health of the nation"; another "attractive packaging". There must be doubts about a phrase capable of so many interpretations.

The danger of vogue words is that they are seen as fashionable and are liable to be paraded by those who may have only a vague idea of what they mean. If they are making a presentation and their audience's comprehension is equally vague, confusion is inevitable. Presenters should steer clear of vogue words unless they are absolutely sure that both they and the audience understand them.

Ambiguity

Danger of misunderstanding arises alike in the words used and the context in which they are used. Some subjects pose particular problems for specific audiences. For example, if an *employer* speaks to an audience of *employees* about job security, they are liable, unless the words (and manner of delivery) are chosen with great care, to assume redundancy is about to be announced.

Words which are close in their sound to other words are easily misunderstood.

> A works manager once told his line managers how important it was to "apprise" their workers (that is, make them aware) of company performance. Many of them thought he was foreshadowing a scheme to "appraise" workers' performance.

When it is impossible to avoid using words that are easily confused with similar ones, it should be made plain from the context exactly what meaning is intended.

Ambiguity is never absolutely unavoidable: some members of some audience at some time are sure to get hold of the wrong end of the stick; but the risk can be considerably reduced with forethought.

Tact

In the seventies it was the job of various Department of Employment officials to spread the gospel about so called productivity schemes. One of them had to address a group of office managers, who proved to be an enlightened and receptive audience, genuinely anxious to improve their operating efficiency. All went well until the official mentioned a valid example of a productivity improvement in a certain Inland Revenue office. The shutters came down at once and the audience switched off from then on. In their mind nothing good was possible on the part of the Inland Revenue and anyone who pretended otherwise was not worth listening to.

Sometimes a presenter has no choice but to speak out bluntly and directness in such circumstances does not equate with tactlessness. But it is foolish to risk closing the ears of the audience to the whole presentation for want of thought about the inclusion or not of some relatively minor passage that might be badly received.

Straightness

Presenters must observe absolute honesty of purpose towards the audience, both in intent and word. To be specific:

(a) do not try to fool the audience with pretentious language
(b) do not try to wriggle out of a difficulty by means of clever talk
(c) do not talk down to the audience.

Presenters should aim to ensure that their listeners' perception of what they say is as near as possible to their intended meaning. They should test the language they propose to use against this standard throughout their preparation and censor anything that fails the test.

Summary

(a) Use language that will be understood by the audience in the sense intended.
(b) Plain language is the means of achieving this, and the words and phrases used should therefore be simple, familiar, unambiguous, tactful and straight.
(c) Complicated sentences should be avoided and jargon, slang, abbreviations and vogue words treated with caution.

Chapter 4
Visual Aids

A visual aid is, by definition, something shown to the audience in order to reinforce and illustrate the presenter's words. In this sense it is subsidiary to, and should not detract from, the impact of either presentation or presenter.

But there are some subjects (for example, an industrial process) which are of necessity heavily dependent on illustration, whether a series of pictures or a film or video. These are not *aids* in the strict sense, as the visual image is central and the spoken words are more a commentary than a presentation. The attention of the audience is mainly on the pictures — and the room may even be darkened to show them to better effect — so that the words play a subsidiary part.

Although the commentary may be comparatively sparse, it has to provide an effective accompaniment to, and its delivery must synchronise with, the pictures. The commentator's main role may be to handle questions and discussion at the end.

If the material is presented frequently, there are good arguments for having a professionally recorded soundtrack.

Circumstances like this, where the presenter, or commentator, takes a secondary and perhaps self-effacing role, may well be more comfortable for nervous people than one where they have to play a more prominent part. The value of visual material as a reassuring prop is discussed later in the chapter and those who have difficulty in conquering nerves might, without overdoing it, derive benefit from making more use of visual aids than is strictly necessary. But the need remains for the presentation (or commentary, if it is better described thus) to be well written and delivered. No visual display, however impressive, can hide an ineffective verbal accompaniment.

At what point the visual display becomes the main focus and the presentation a commentary is a matter of degree and there are certainly circumstances where a comparatively large number of visual aids are required in concert with what properly remains a presentation.

A plant engineer was giving a presentation about a manufacturing process. He happened to be a talented artist and had expertly sketched on flip-chart sheets a succession of diagrams, without which his explanation of the process, good as it was, would have been difficult to follow. His words still amounted to a presentation, as his presence in front of his audience gave it an authority it would otherwise have lacked. The fact that his audience were aware that the drawings were his own work also no doubt strengthened the impact he made.

This was a comparatively rare instance of a true presentation requiring a good deal of visual material. As a general rule, too many visual aids distract rather than assist and for some presentations visual aids are neither necessary nor appropriate. It is wise to use only those visual aids that serve a clear purpose and guard against over-dependence, as circumstances can sometimes reduce their effectiveness (for example when strong sunlight in a room without curtains makes an overhead projector almost useless).

Nevertheless, visual aids are more often than not useful adjuncts. Their value as a means of illustration or emphasis is obvious. If a presenter wishes, for example, to explain a sales trend, a graph or bar chart will indicate the position more clearly than any words. If it is desirable to emphasise a particular word or phrase, repeating it visually impresses its importance on the audience. In many ways eyes are more receptive to a message than ears.

Apart from their intrinsic usefulness, however, visual aids have some indirect advantages. In the first place, they are, as already mentioned, useful as a prop. Practical people are often more comfortable with the tangible than the intangible and many of them feel isolated when left alone with the spoken word. To a nervous presenter a visual aid can be a real ally.

The general manager of a company manufacturing surgical equipment had to make a presentation describing his factory and was at first painfully stiff and self-conscious. Happily, after a few minutes he delved into his brief case and produced one of his products. He put it on the table beside him and went on with some aplomb to describe its manufacture and use, just touching it from time to time to point out one of its features. Contact with something familiar, which in an important way assisted his presentation, gave him the prop he obviously needed.

Secondly, bringing a visual aid into use can provide a legitimate reason for a pause in the flow of words. Pauses, in their appropriate places (to be discussed in due course), play an important part in making an effective presentation — all the better when they appear to have an obvious purpose; there is none better than to introduce a visual aid.

The third incidental advantage of visual aids is that they can make movement purposeful. Movement (also to be dealt with later) introduces variety into a presentation and when it has a purpose there is much less risk of awkwardness.

General Rules about Visual Aids

(a) Effective operation of visual aids requires practice.
(b) It is worthwhile, if it can be done without detriment to the presentation, to space out their use, so that the incidental pauses and movements are evenly spread.
(c) Check beforehand that equipment is in working order, conveniently placed and stable and that the image the audience will see is visible and legible.
(d) Keep visual aids simple and brief. Many, including some produced professionally, are unnecessarily elaborate, often with a profusion of colours and decoration which obscure the message.
(e) Stand back from the image (unless something has to be pointed out) in order to give the impression that it is there for the presenters' benefit as much as for the audience's.
(f) Be silent for a time after displaying a visual aid, so that the audience have a chance to assimilate it. Do not read out what the audience can read for themselves. A brief comment or summary of the visual message is sufficient.

(g) Do not use a visual aid merely because it happens to be available. There may be occasions when the presentation is going so well and the audience is so intent that to interrupt the flow with a visual aid, however apt, might be counter-productive.
(h) Do not lose contact with the audience while setting up a visual aid. An occasional smile or a word or two keeps the presenter in touch.
(i) Having finished with a visual aid, remove it and switch off any equipment.

Flip Charts, Blackboards and Whiteboards

These have the common characteristic that they do not have to be prepared in advance and therefore have an immediacy not shared by other visual aids. They can be brought into use spontaneously and do not need projection equipment.

Blackboards, using chalk, and whiteboards, using felt markers, require no explanation. Useful as both are, they have the disadvantage that, unless erased and therefore lost for ever, what has been written remains visible and a potential distraction when the presenter moves on to another topic.

Flip charts are large pads of paper, mounted on an easel and used with a felt marker. When the presenter has finished with one sheet, it can be turned over, so that what has been written is hidden, but recoverable if it is necessary to refer to it again. Material can, of course, also be prepared in advance and left covered until needed. Doing this can, if skilfully timed, have quite a dramatic effect.

The managing director of a pharmaceutical company was describing the disadvantages of conventional methods of administering eye-drops. He then announced, with a flourish: "And this is our answer!", simultaneously turning over the flip chart sheet to reveal an illustration of a revolutionary new development in eye-drop delivery.

Many experienced presenters have said that if they were allowed only one piece of visual aid equipment they would choose a flip chart, as being the simplest and most versatile of such tools. The following advice may help to get the best out of it.

(a) Carry some spare felt markers in case the ones provided have dried up. Put the top back on markers when not in use to keep them moist.
(b) Presenters who are right handed should stand to the right of the flip chart (the audience's left) and the opposite if they are left handed. This allows better contact with the audience than if the back is turned completely when writing. The easel may be moved, if necessary.
(c) Write neatly, boldly and large enough to be legible from the back of the audience. This is easier said than done, so it is worthwhile putting in some practice. Use printed or block letters rather than longhand, space the writing generously and guard against a tendency (to which many are prone) for a line of writing to slope downwards as it approaches the far margin.
(d) If there is anything at all complicated to put up (for example, a graph), faintly pencil in an outline beforehand. A pencilled-in horizontal guide line is similarly useful for a person who cannot write straight. The audience will not be able to see these faint marks.
(e) Be brief — three or four key words are more comprehensible (and easier to write out) than a full sentence and a simple diagram is preferable to a complicated one.
(f) Do not allow a sheet to get cluttered. Turn it over after making one point, so that a clean sheet is ready for the next.
(g) The one disadvantage of a flip-chart is that in a large hall even the largest writing may not be visible from the back. Check this beforehand.

Overhead Projector (OHP)

This widely used equipment enables an image, inscribed with a felt pen or photocopied on an acetate sheet, to be projected on a screen. Some OHPs incorporate an acetate roll but to write on it a presenter has to perch uncomfortably over the OHP in such a way that it is difficult to maintain contact with the audience.

A mathematician once delivered a lecture from a seat over the OHP, on which he inscribed an incessant series of equations. Perhaps fellow mathematicians were sufficiently interested in his equations to ignore the fact that he hardly looked at them, but many of the lay members of the audience were obviously uncomfortable.

For practical purposes the OHP requires advance preparation of acetates. Acetates are available in cardboard frames, which may be easier to handle and keep in sequence, but they are more expensive and bulkier to carry around. Many presenters prefer unframed acetates. Framed or unframed, it is useful to number them in sequence. If the acetates do get out of sequence, keep calm: audiences are tolerant of minor hitches, but can become impatient with a presenter who gets unduly flustered.

The hallmarks of a good OHP, as of any visual aid, are neatness, clarity and brevity. With practice, most people can achieve this freehand with a suitable felt pen. Better results are usually obtained by working against a lined backing, although pads of acetates interleaved with squared paper are also obtainable. Do not try to cover too much on one acetate. Use short, pithy phrases or (even better) single words, if they convey the message adequately. Diagrams are best sketched out on paper first, then traced on an acetate. Skilled help may be needed if diagrams are complicated and they should in any case be as simple as possible.

An alternative to freehand printing is to type the image on A4 paper, using the largest available lettering, then photocopy it on an acetate sheet, enlarging the image as necessary to a sufficient size. Take care over this: typed lettering too small to be seen from the back is a common fault.

Existing documents can, of course, be photocopied on acetates, but this should be done *only where they are suitable for display to an audience*. Material such as balance sheets, sales figures, technical diagrams, graphs and tables can usefully illuminate a speech, but they are usually designed in their original form for comparatively leisurely perusal. To be useful as visual aids they probably have to be redesigned or summarised.

An official was making a presentation about some new legislation, using photocopied pages of the relevant Act as visual aids. To make matters worse, she then proceeded to quote large chunks from the text: a classic model of how *not* to use a visual aid!

Some presenters use visual aids as notes. This is perfectly acceptable if they are confident and know their subject well enough to need no more than a few words or a simple diagram on the screen as a reminder. But those who feel more comfortable with reasonably comprehensive notes would require something too elaborate to be a useful visual aid.

Visual aids should not be used as notes except by presenters who are certain they can perform convincingly with no more prompting than a relatively sparse visual layout.

There is a common habit of masking the OHP display with a slip of paper and revealing it to the audience bit by bit, on the ground presumably that if the whole image is exposed their attention will wander from the current point. But this often has the reverse effect, as it is a natural reaction to wonder what lies concealed. For this reason many experienced presenters see no value in masking part of the image.

If it is necessary to point anything out, point to the image on the screen rather than to the acetate on the platform of the OHP, thus pointing to the image the *audience* can see, rather than to the source of the image, which they cannot see.

Display Charts

Display charts are useful for displaying non-verbal material, such as plans, diagrams and graphs. For purposes of this kind they are probably better than OHP acetates. But, even more than acetates, they need skilled draughtsmanship, as well as suitable materials and adequate time for preparation, which are not always available. An easel or stand is, of course, required to put them on.

Films and Videos

Films and videos are not strictly visual aids in the sense in which the term is used in this guide. There may, however, be circumstances where short clips from films or videos are appropriate in conjunction with a presentation. Their handling has to be slick and well timed, which requires practice. This form of visual aid should not be used unless the presenter is sure it is going to work well.

A film or video can occasionally be used quite effectively as an interlude. (It has, of course, to be appropriate and complementary to the content of the presentation and again its use has to be well timed.)

Photographic Transparencies

Transparencies need a projector, which is usually located at a distance from the presenter, so that it has to be operated either by an assistant or by remote control. Care is needed not to cast a shadow on the screen and the room may sometimes have to be darkened.

A series of transparencies may be essential to the presentation: a lecture on some architectural subject is a good example. But, if a few transparencies are used as intermittent visual aids, they may not be worth the trouble.

Physical Objects

A piece of equipment or a manufactured product may be a useful backdrop and, if familiar to the presenter, a source of confidence. If it is the subject of the presentation, it may be virtually essential. Hand it around, if this adds to the interest, but remember that passing anything around the audience takes time and tends to distract attention from what is being said, so make allowances accordingly. (Handing things around is not usually feasible if there is a large audience.)

Handouts

Handouts used as visual aids, as distinct from reminder handouts, which are dealt with in the next section, should be brief, clear, easily assimilable, and illuminate a single and simple point. If it is possible to achieve the same purpose with a chart or OHP, it is better to use them, as anything in the hands of the audience that has to be read is a potential distraction.

Handouts can, however, be appropriate visual aids where there is a small, interested and committed audience. In a sales presentation, for example, a brief handout summary, preferably on a single sheet of paper, of the claims made for the product can make a good impression, better perhaps than a summary on a flip-chart or screen. As a means of emphasising a single, decisive point, a handout may, in the right circumstances, have unique advantages over other methods.

A consultant *started* his presentation by distributing a handout, on which were set out three questions he asked his audience to consider. In this case a handout was probably the best method of concentrating each person's attention. The subsequent presentation consisted substantially in discussing the answers — but the consultant probably had a good idea beforehand of what the answers were going to be.

Reminder Handouts

Handouts intended as a reminder should, for obvious reasons, be issued *after*, not during or before a presentation.

They serve a useful purpose in a business presentation in that they provide the audience with an accurate record of what has been said (although some members may also wish to make their own notes). A presenter who is going to issue a handout should announce this intention at the beginning.

The form of a handout is to some extent predetermined by its purpose. A sales presentation may, for example, be followed by the distribution of promotional material or a financial analysis by a set of accounts. Some handouts may be elaborate and extensive, intended to have a prestige value, although the recipients may sometimes lose sight of the wood for the luxuriance of the trees. Presenters have to be clear about their real purpose: do they wish the presentation itself to be remembered or is it merely a formality, intended primarily to launch the handout? If the presentation is intended to have priority, a simpler handout may do the job better.

The following suggestions may help in preparing reminder handouts.

(a) Handouts should be specially designed for their particular purpose.
(b) Existing documents usually require adaptation.
(c) A handout should look good.
(d) It should be clear, simple and easy to read, with nothing extraneous and the main points accurately and pithily set out.
(e) A copy of the presenter's script, whatever its form, is unlikely to be suitable (unless it is a prepared text, intended for publication).
(f) Statistical or financial data, unless confined to a simple statement, are best put in an appendix.

The preparation of handouts calls for care, imagination, and fluent, taut and grammatical prose. Presenters who have any doubts about their ability with the pen should get help or at least ask someone to go over their draft.

Summary

(a) The aim of visual aids is to emphasise or illustrate points in the presentation; do not use too many.
(b) If the visual display is the main focus of attention, the spoken words that accompany it are more a commentary.
(c) A visual aid has a useful incidental role as a prop for the presenter or a natural opportunity for pausing or moving.
(d) Practise using visual aids and check beforehand that equipment is conveniently positioned and in good working order.
(e) Visual aids should be simple, neat, comprehensible and visible.
(f) The audience should be given time to take them in.
(g) Visual aids should not be used unnecessarily, simply because they happen to be available.
(h) Switch off equipment after each use.
(i) Flip charts are good general purpose visual aids, which can be used impromptu, but OHPs, although also versatile, require acetates which generally have to be prepared in advance.
(j) Existing documents can be photocopied on acetates, but are usually too detailed to make successful visual aids.
(k) Masking part of the OHP image is of dubious value.
(l) If it is necessary to point anything out, point at the image on the screen.
(m) Using visual aids as notes needs experience and skill.
(n) Display charts are the best medium for non-verbal material, but usually need skilled advance preparation.
(o) Films and videos are a separate medium of communication and are not usually appropriate in conjunction with presentations.
(p) In the right circumstances, a physical object can be an effective visual aid.
(q) Simple handouts are sometimes appropriate as visual aids, but are a potential distraction.
(r) Any reminder handout should be issued *after* the presentation.
(s) The audience should be informed at the start if a reminder handout is to be issued.

(t) Handouts should be clear, simple and easy to read. Reproductions of existing material are often unsatisfactory.

Chapter 5
The Script

To capture and retain the attention of the audience, presenters must aim to make their presentation appear as natural and immediate as possible. They must try to convey the impression that their words are designed especially for that particular group of people.

Reading from a text is unlikely to achieve this, except in skilled hands. At the same time, most presenters need a memory jogger, ideally a script which is an effective reminder but not so precise as to inhibit spontaneity.

The majority of experienced presenters find that notes are the most satisfactory form of script and the greater part of this chapter is devoted to their preparation and use.

But the alternatives must also be considered: namely reading word for word, from either manuscript or autocue, and learning the text by heart.

Reading from the Manuscript

Most presenters who follow their script word for word make it obvious that they are reading, and spontaneity and rapport are thereby at risk. Furthermore, they have little practical choice but to stick to the script; it is hard to change anything should it become evident that the needs of the audience have been miscalculated.

Reading is, of course, sometimes a necessity. Prominent people, such as politicians, who have to make a great many speeches, often have little choice. Their text will frequently have been written by aides and they may have too little time to study it more than cursorily beforehand. Material that is sensitive or likely to be reported may also have to be read word for word.

Some in this position are admirable readers, well able to grip their audience with the power of their delivery and feeling for language (Winston Churchill, for example), quite apart from the interest of their words. The existence of such models cannot, however, be allowed to obscure the fact that comparatively few of the prominent people who regularly read their text word for word make a particularly good job of it. Still fewer amateurs have the necessary skill and reading is a non-starter in the great majority of business presentations. The only exceptions might be public speeches by senior executives, who in these circumstances come within the category of "prominent people", and announcements of such importance or sensitivity that they must be word perfect. An example of the latter is where a policy announcement has to be made by several people simultaneously and it is vital that an identical message is conveyed by all: spontaneity has then to be sacrificed to certainty.

Those who are obliged to or insist that they must read a presentation, should try, at any rate, to deliver it as convincingly, interestingly and if the occasion demands, forcefully as possible. This requires practice, but it is also possible to make things easier by setting out the text in a way that brings out the sense and cadence of the words.

Take the sentence: "We are a successful company because we try harder than our competitors". To get the best out of the sentence the words "successful", "try" and "competitors" should be emphasised and there should be pause after "company". The layout of the text can help to make this clear, thus:

"We are a *successful* [EMPHASISE] company [PAUSE]

because we *try* harder than our *competitors*."

The two things to bring out are emphasis and pauses and these have to be calculated during preparation and incorporated in whatever layout best suits the individual. The above example indicates emphasis by means of italics, but underlining, block letters or coloured lettering will serve just as well. Pauses can be conveniently indicated by starting a new line at the appropriate point. One of the dangers of thus setting out the text, however, is that it can lead to a staccato delivery, another good reason why practice is essential.

In short, reading from the full text is not a soft option and requires much application if it is to be done effectively. But most presenters, however hard they work at it, are more likely to gain immediacy and impact if they use notes.

Autocue

Autocue is a device much used in television and sometimes called an "idiot board". But it is far from being a refuge for idiots: it is full of hazards, even for those practised in its use.

The text unfolds on a monitor, out of sight of the audience, so that the presenter has to stand behind a lectern. In an up-to-date variant, the monitor appears to the audience as a transparent screen and is much less noticeable.

Television is, of course, a different matter from a live presentation. In the former, the audience, from the presenter's point of view, is the camera and, as the autocue is in front of it, viewers have the impression that the presenter is looking directly at them. There is no such convenient proximity in the case of a live audience.

Autocue requires too much equipment to be used frequently in business presentations, but there are from time to time staged events, such as sales conferences and shareholder meetings, where autocue may well be appropriate and it is therefore worthwhile to discuss its use.

There are two problems. The first is that the presenter *appears* to have no script, with the implication that the presentation is spontaneous. But the presenter is, in fact, reading, so that, unless this is done well, the illusion of spontaneity is dispelled, leaving the audience with an impression of a dull performer, ill at ease with the material.

The second problem is that the presenter is tied to the monitor and cannot escape from behind the lectern. An impression of rigidity is inevitable unless eye contact and head gesture compensate adequately for lack of body movement. The presenter therefore has a difficult task, in view of the need for the eye to follow the monitor.

Autocue was installed at a trade union conference. One official, a practised speaker, who prides himself on his ability to achieve rapport with his audience, tried his hand at it, but soon became so exasperated by its constraints that he gave it up and reverted to his notes (which he fortunately had by him in reserve).

It would be wrong to decry an aid which is most useful in expert hands in the right circumstances, but effective use requires experience, thorough preparation and, possibly, tuition. And for those who, despite practice, are unable to achieve a happy balance of attention between audience and monitor it is better left alone.

Learning by Heart

Learning a text by heart and attempting to repeat it word for word is full of hazards and should not be contemplated, except perhaps for short, informal addresses, say of thanks or welcome. Anything more requires such an effort of memory, with the attendant risk of forgetting one's lines, that it is not a worthwhile option.

It is pointless to make a comparison with the long stretches of words stage performers have to learn by heart. These people are professionals, with the advantages of getting cues from their colleagues and, if they forget their lines (a not infrequent occurrence), the help of a prompter.

In a business environment, it would be ridiculous to take a prompter when making a presentation, but, without this assistance, the effort of concentration needed to recall the words would be beyond most presenters and would for many result in a mechanical delivery, with little expression or animation.

There is, however, one method of memorising a presentation used by those who have the necessary confidence. This amounts to memorising, not every word, but the *framework* of the presentation, which is then delivered as though from notes — in practice, it is the notes that have been memorised. Except for those few gifted with photographic memories, the method becomes a possibility only when the same presentation is made several times and the subject matter can be recalled without conscious effort.

To make a deliberate attempt to master this technique would be unwise. Some presenters may, however, find, after making a presentation on the same subject a few times, that they can perform confidently without referring to their notes; what it amounts to is that they grow into dispensing with notes rather than do so deliberately. The test is whether they feel more comfortable and can perform better without notes than with notes. Perhaps a halfway house is best, referring to notes only occasionally, particularly to check the time or as a means of rescuing oneself in an emergency. The last thing presenters should do is to dispense with notes completely. Having them close at hand will maintain their confidence in their ability to manage without them.

Dispensing with a script should not be attempted unless presenters have a reasonable amount of experience and complete confidence in their ability to carry it off. It should never be done just to show off.

Notes

Many presenters underestimate their ability to speak from notes. Notes are the commonest and, on almost all counts, most satisfactory script for presenters and those who lack confidence in their use should not be deterred by feelings of unease in the early stages.

Notes are nothing more than a series of memory joggers to remind presenters of their text. How fully and in what manner they are set out is a matter of personal choice and presenters learn from experience which layout suits them best and usually chop and change before settling for one or other. Some presenters need only a word or two to remind them of each point; others prefer more detail. The latter may find it useful to distinguish the salient points by means of underlining or using different coloured lettering.

The following example is one way of preparing notes for a short passage in an imaginary sales presentation. Here is the text: "What I want to do next is to tell you about some of the many advantages of our new product. The first will already be obvious: because of its size and convenient shape it is very easy to handle and also to carry, be it in pocket or handbag. You may also notice that it has a distinctive colour — to aid instant recognition. The third advantage is less obvious, but I can assure you that it is the most durable product of its kind now on the market; this has been proved after extensive user tests. And finally the price — very competitive indeed and even cheaper than a number of its distinctly inferior rivals."

Notes for the above passage might be:
"Advantages = size — shape — OK handbag or pocket — colour —
durability — favourable price"

A confident presenter might need no more than:
"Advantages = size — shape — durability — price"

Or if particularly well-practised, merely:
"Advantages"

Another matter for personal preference is whether notes are written on paper or, as many prefer, on cards (usually about 6″×4″). The advantage of such cards is their handy size, rigidity and the fact that they are easily held without impeding hand and arm movement. Against that, it is not possible to get much writing of reasonable size on a comparatively small card (a larger card is cumbersome).

A4 paper, although not so handy, can accommodate a good amount of writing on each sheet, so that the notes can be better viewed as a whole. Some presenters go half way and use A5 paper. But, size apart, it is unwise to use paper that is too flimsy and thus liable to crumple.

Notes, whether on cards or paper, should be numbered in sequence, so that if they are dropped or get mixed up they can be put back in order with the minimum of fuss. A surprising number of experienced speakers fail to do this, perhaps taking the line, "It can't happen to me". But it can! Some presenters find it hard to recover their poise after such a mishap. An additional precaution is to fix the cards or sheets together.

It is useful to differentiate in some way (underlining or coloured ink) between essential points, non-essential points and anecdotes or illustrations. This enables a presenter who is running behind time to identify quickly material that can be discarded. A marginal note about any visual aid is a further worthwhile signpost.

It is necessary for presenters to keep a check on the passage of time in order to know when to make adjustments. This can be done relatively easily by entering a guide time at various stages in the notes, worked out during rehearsal.

The opening and closing passages, as well as any particularly apposite phrases the presenter does not wish to forget, should, of course, be written out in full.

Apart from material that can, if necessary, be discarded, it is also useful to have reserve material available, in case, contrary to expectations, there is a gap to fill. Keeping reserve material in the main body of the notes, however, adds to the difficulty of seeing the wood for the trees. It is usually more convenient to have a separate appendix containing such standby items as discarded non-essential points, extra anecdotes and any odd bits of factual and background information that may be helpful in replying to questions (anticipating which is a matter for a later chapter). Another useful item to have is a list of the names of the more important people in the audience (which can be ascertained if they are not known). Presenters score marks with the audience if they can refer to one or two of its members by name and it can be acutely embarrassing to forget a name which ought to be familiar.

Finally, make sure that the notes are readable: that they are neatly and legibly written, in good sized lettering. If a presenter's handwriting is untidy, the notes should be typed (but make sure the typist knows how to set them out).

Using Notes

The first attribute of notes is that, systematically arranged, they provide an immediately accessible "map" of the presentation, guiding presenters in their chosen direction and enabling them to retrace their steps if they get lost.

The second is that, apart from their opening and closing passages and any phrases they feel will make an impact at some appropriate point, presenters are not tied to a particular form of words.

The third aspect of notes is that it is possible, relatively easily, to make minor variations from the original sequence, if necessary. This contingency might occur, for example, if it appeared better to bring forward some explanatory material intended to be introduced later or held in reserve. A word for word narrative is not nearly so flexible.

Notes are the servant of the presenter, unlike a full text, which, because of its very purpose, allows little or no scope for variation.

The following suggestions about the use of notes may be helpful.

(a) Except on the rare occasions when there is no choice but to depart radically from the script, it is better to stick to the framework of the notes and not diverge unless it is done consciously and purposefully. Inexperienced presenters commonly come to the end of their performance unaware of what they have been saying and oblivious of their notes. It is necessary for presenters to make a determined effort to follow their notes and exercising this discipline will make them feel a good deal more in command of the situation.

(b) Presenters who lose their place, should pause and search for it as calmly as possible. The audience are more likely than not to be unaware of it, whereas any agitation apparent in the presenter will almost certainly be noticed.

(c) Occasionally check the time against the guide time on the notes and adjust accordingly (perhaps discarding material or using reserve material) if the presentation is significantly adrift. This is not always easy for a beginner, but it becomes second nature with practice.

(d) Do not *read* from the notes (except for the opening or closing passage or any special phrases, if memory fails). Notes are not meant to be read out: they are for the benefit of the presenter, not the audience. While there should be no attempt to conceal notes, they are better unacknowledged. In this way they will be taken for granted by the audience.

(e) Familiarity with the layout of the notes enables the presenter to know exactly where to find a particular reference. If it is then necessary to refer to some point out of the sequence originally intended, it should be possible to do so without hesitation.

(f) Presenters get to know with experience the most comfortable place for their notes. If they are kept in the hand (a great advantage of 6″ × 4″ cards), it is better not to "cuddle" them, an attitude which tends to constrict the body and appear defensive. Notes should be held as an extension of the hand and if the hand is used to make a gesture the notes should move with it.

Holding the notes in hand can be a problem if presenters wish to use a visual aid, particularly a flip-chart. In this case it is better to put the notes down for the time being. Many presenters in any case leave their notes on a table beside them, picking them up from time to time as they wish. This need not inhibit movement: presenters separated from their notes who wish to refer to them need only move back calmly to where they have been left (an example of "purposeful" movement).

A student at a tutorial had moved towards the audience as a perfectly legitimate gesture of emphasis. But she then found herself "marooned". "What shall I do?" she asked the tutor. "Move back to your notes and have a look at them," she was told. It was the obvious and natural thing to do, but until she was "given permission" she lacked the confidence to act naturally. Her confidence all round grew from this point and she went on to become an accomplished presenter.

It is important for presenters to get used to handling notes naturally and not think of them as inhibiting movement or a barrier between themselves and the audience. Notes should be treated as though they were a natural appendage, as a pop singer handles a microphone, without any embarrassment or furtiveness.

Summary

(a) Reading word for word is inflexible and few presenters have the skill to do it without loss of expression. If it is necessary to read, the text should be set out in a way that brings out the cadence and emphasis of the words.
(b) Autocue tends to induce rigidity and lack of warmth, unless used expertly.
(c) Learning the text by heart is too risky to be acceptable. Exceptionally, some experienced presenters are able to commit the *framework* of the text to memory and speak as though from notes.
(d) Notes are the best form of script for most people.
(e) Set them out neatly, generously spaced and legibly, with salient points highlighted.
(f) Number the cards or sheets in sequence.
(g) Enter a guide-time at intervals.
(h) Include key names and reserve material in an appendix.
(i) Familiarity with the layout of the notes enables them to be used with maximum flexibility.
(k) Notes should be handled without self-consciousness and as though they were a natural accessory.

Chapter 6
Delivery

The best of material, however carefully prepared, can be spoiled by poor delivery, and imperfect material can sometimes be saved by good delivery. For one who is not reasonably gifted by nature, eloquent delivery is the aspect of presentation that is the most difficult to acquire. But it is an art that can be mastered to a reasonable degree by all but the very few. Only the rudiments can be learned from a book, however; the rest is a matter of practice.

The purpose of good delivery is to make the most favourable and effective impact on the audience. The importance of the audience is paramount.

The Audience

Presenters, however expert or prestigious, who believe they can command automatic attention from an audience, however committed or awestruck, can expect sooner or later to be disappointed. Some presenters are, it is true, sufficiently magnetic, interesting or amusing to be able to hold an audience most of the time and some audiences are more attentive than a presenter deserves. Sometimes these exceptional presenters and audiences coincide, but even then 100 per cent attention is so rare that it can, for practical purposes, be discounted. Audiences always have extraneous, possibly trivial, matters on their minds, which impinge intermittently. This is especially so in business situations, where those in the audience may have left one or more priority matters in order to listen to the presentation and expect to return when it is over to other compelling responsibilities.

Attention is most likely to be ensured by presenters who make audiences feel comfortable and give them confidence that they are going to hear something worthwhile. They look forward to presenters being well prepared, capable of dealing with whatever crops up and not likely to waste their time.

A business audience is not going to expect great flights of oratory and business presenters should not attempt more than they can deliver. They should not put themselves in a position where, in the words of a film line, "Your ego is writing cheques your body can't cash".

First impressions are vital. If favourable, there is a store of goodwill that can be drawn on if anything goes wrong later. If it is poor, it can diminish the impact of what follows and the presenter must work that much harder to get a response.

Presenters should look their best, dress attractively without going over the top and take some pains with grooming. They should move smartly, but without hurrying.

Is it better to sit or stand? Some presenters favour sitting, which they say puts them more on terms with the audience and helps them to relax. This is reasonable enough, provided their real motive is not a wish to hide — to make themselves a smaller target, as it were. They should face the audience as though they *expect* to be listened to and convey the impression that they have something worthwhile to impart. It is difficult to do this from a sitting position and it is preferable, therefore, for them to begin on their feet, whatever happens afterwards.

Many lecture rooms are designed to isolate presenters, who are expected to address the audience from behind a table or, worse still, a lectern. Any advantages these may have tend to be outweighed by the fact that they constitute a *barrier* between presenter and audience: a barrier which can only make it more difficult to establish rapport between the two. Presenters who are confronted with either a table or lectern are well advised to move to one side of it, so that they face the audience unobstructed. Many presenters favour having a small table on their left, which leaves them face to face with the audience (with somewhere to put their notes) and free to move about if they wish.

In business situations, of course, presenters often have to perform where they find themselves, but it is as well to know the layout they prefer, so that they can position themselves to the best advantage.

The best place for the person in the chair, if any, is with the audience, once the introductions are over. It is worth having a word beforehand and suggesting — without, of course, making an issue of it — that it is better for a presenter to face the audience alone. (In Chapter 6 there is a discussion of the part the occupant of the chair should play during question time.)

Presenters should not start talking before they are in position. If they have to walk any distance to get to the front, there is no reason not to look (amiably) at the audience, but without saying anything. Once they are in place they have two immediate tasks. First, they have to gain the audience's attention and, secondly, they have to allow a few seconds for a mutual examination, an action which helps to set up an immediate relationship. Presenters should stand up straight, relaxed and still; smile and look as though they are pleased to be there. If they occasionally have to wait to get attention, they should continue to look at the audience and keep still (apart from head and eyes) and silent until they have the attention of all.

Salutation

How should a presenter address the audience? Nowadays almost any salutation has its perils, but "ladies and gentlemen", although it may sound a bit stilted, is safe for most occasions. (Avoid "lady and gentlemen". "Ms Smith and gentlemen" is preferable if there is only one woman present – it is usually possible to find out her name; the reverse of course if there is only one man present.) If in doubt, however, leave it at "thank you, good morning".

Introductory Words

A short, arresting, punchy introductory sentence or two, prepared beforehand, as already suggested, has the effect of reinforcing the attention gained and, equally importantly, arousing the expectations of the audience, so that they are alert for what is to follow.

Confidence

It is important to convey to the audience an impression of confidence. Presenters may quite often have to steel themselves to portray an air of assurance they do not necessarily feel, but they will find that confidence is self-reinforcing; the audience will sense and react accordingly to a presenter who clearly expects to be listened to.

It can be a particular trial for a presenter who has reason to be apprehensive about the reaction of one or more individual members of the audience (the boss or a key customer, perhaps). The best course is to acknowledge their status, without being obsequious, and thereafter treat them merely as part of the audience at large. To direct attention too obviously at them is liable to cause mutual embarrassment.

Eye Contact

Eyes play an essential part in the process of communication. But it is not sufficient for presenters to look in the *general* direction of the audience: they have to move their eyes from individual to individual (an action which has the incidental benefit of relaxing neck and head muscles) and thus establish direct overall contact. They must not be deterred by self-consciousness, the likelihood that some will avert their eyes, or the ever present temptation to look at the wall, the ceiling, the floor — anywhere but at the audience. Presenters who find their eyes wandering should direct them back to the audience, not abruptly, but in easy stages, perhaps via their notes.

Persevere with the Audience

An audience's intitial reaction can be at best cautious and an apparent absence of response can be disconcerting. It is essential not to be discouraged; provided what presenters say makes sense and they say it with conviction, they will break through any reserve and feel an increasing sense of warming towards them. Presenters must, by their demeanour, make it plain that they *want* and *expect* the audience to listen.

One presenter actually said. "I have to give this talk and you have to listen to it, so let's get it over as quickly as possible". It so happened he had some interesting material, but few bothered to listen; those fatal words had switched most of them off.

Intelligibility

The point was made in Chapter 3 (Language) that there is a potential gap between the presenter's intentions and the listener's perceptions. But appropriate choice of words is not enough, as audiences do not pay attention all the time and may therefore mishear or miss altogether key parts of the presentation. Failure to absorb even a few words may make the difference between understanding and misunderstanding. It is the presenter's job to ensure that the attention of the listener is directed at the words that matter and that these words are interpreted accurately. The aim is minimum misunderstanding and maximum intelligibility, the means of achieving which are:

(a) paragraphing
(b) signposting and
(c) emphasis.

Paragraphing

This is a simple and obvious concept. It means only that presenters make it clear to the audience when they have completed one stage and are moving on to another. To run on without putting up a signal that they are on a different tack can leave the audience confused and liable to lose concentration. An example of paragraphing would be "Having dealt with 'A', I am now going to tell you about 'B' ".

Signposting

A signpost directs the attention of the audience to something worthy of notice. It may be a pause, a gesture, a change of inflection or volume, or some other signal. Presenters learn to select whatever is appropriate at the time.

> One schoolteacher, when he came to a significant point, used to take off his glasses, beam at the class and say slowly, "Now . . ." and everyone knew they were expected to listen hard.

Emphasis

Emphasis gives life and punch to language and its dramatic effect is only half its usefulness. Emphasis also plays an indispensable part in enhancing intelligibility. Incorrect emphasis can obscure the meaning of a passage and, even if the meaning is obvious from the context, correct emphasis makes it easier for the listener to grasp its drift. Anything that simplifies the task of the listener automatically simplifies the task of the presenter.

Emphasis is usually achieved by *stressing* significant words (or syllables), as in the following example.

Take the sentence: "I will help you". Note how the meaning changes as the stress is transferred from one word to the next.

"*I* will help you." [*I*, and nobody else.]
"I *will* help you." [You may rely on me to help you.]
"I will *help* you." [*Help*, and not deter.]
"I will help *you*." [*You*, and nobody else.]

Another form of emphasis is *inflexion*.

The words: "Not tonight, Josephine [his Empress]." are commonly attributed to Napoleon. Inflected as a statement, they indicate that Josephine has made a proposal, which he has declined. But turn the words into a question: "Not tonight, Josephine?" and the roles are reversed; Napoleon becomes the proposer and Josephine the dissenter.

Correct emphasis tends to come naturally in everyday conversation, but presenters sometimes forget it when they are perhaps a bit keyed up in a formal situation. The solution is experience and practice, which give them the confidence to relax, so that their natural feeling for words can reassert itself.

Even professionals do not always get it right, however, and television and radio performers are frequent culprits. In trying to get some punch into their delivery, a few of them contrive to put the emphasis in quite the wrong place, sometimes with odd results.

> A television reporter referred to the riot at "Strangeways *prison*" (in order, perhaps, not to confuse it with some other building in the area).

Interest

Interest goes hand in hand with intelligibility. An intelligible text, intelligibly delivered, is likely of itself to be interesting; while anything interesting assists intelligibility, in that the audience is thereby more likely to *listen*. This is why interesting anecdotes are such an important part of the text.

The interest of the audience is immediately aroused by presenters whose delivery has decision and bite: who appear to believe what they say. Of necessity their delivery has to be slightly overstressed, compared with what is usual in conversation and they may at first feel self-conscious about this, since, if they go too far, they can appear theatrical. But it has to be remembered that, unlike conversation, a presentation is actually a *performance* and requires presenters to make an effort to punch home their words. (There are some people who make their conversation a performance: oddly enough, they are often as inhibited as anyone else when it comes to a presentation.)

An intelligibly and interestingly delivered presentation has much in common with telling a story effectively. Both make use of certain well tried devices, namely:

(a) variation of pitch and pace
(b) pausing
(c) linking phrases and rhetorical questions
(d) repetition and
(e) summarising.

All these are interrelated and often used in combination.

Variation of Pitch and Pace

Nothing is more likely to switch off the audience than a presentation delivered in a monotone or at an even pace, whether slow or fast. To raise (or lower) the voice or to speak faster (or slower), on the other hand, wakes up the audience and induces a sense of anticipation. Variation of pitch and pace makes for an alert and interested audience and is particularly valuable as a means of signposting and emphasis.

Pausing

Pausing gives the audience time to absorb what is being said. However clearly presenters express themselves, the audience, even if alert and quick on the uptake, need time to assimilate one idea before taking in the next. A pause is especially useful if something significant is being dealt with, a short pause before and after having the effect of isolating, and thus emphasising, that particular passage and underlining its significance.

Apart from its value in assisting intelligibility, pausing is an invaluable ingredient in enhancing both interest and dramatic effect.

Winston Churchill made masterly use of the pause. The following passage occurred during one of his greatest war time speeches (in Ottawa on 30.12.41):

". . . [the French] told their Prime Minister and his divided Cabinet, 'In three weeks England will have her neck wrung like a chicken'. Some chicken; some neck."

This is how he delivered it:

". . . told their Prime Minister . . . 'In three weeks England will have her neck wrung like a chicken'. [two second *pause*] Some chicken; [two second *pause*] some neck." [*stress* on "neck"]

Those who have seen the film of this speech will recall the mischievous twinkle in his eye and the spontaneous delight of the distinguished audience at the last four words of this passage.

Linking Phrases and Rhetorical Questions

Pausing, if overdone, can become tedious and it is therefore useful to be able to "fill" a necessary pause with something which is positive but not in itself significant. Fortunately this is available in the shape of the *linking phrase (or word)* and the *rhetorical question*. Apart from their use as substitutes for a pause, both have a valuable role as a means of paragraphing, signposting and emphasis. The link (for short) may be a single word, such as "and", "but" or "however", spoken slowly and with appropriate weight, so that the audience is led to expect the next passage to be worth paying attention to. Equally, it can be a phase, such as "now comes something that may surprise you" or "let us now turn to the next development" or the commonplace but none the less effective "so much for A — now let's turn to B".

President Bush used the link very effectively in the course of a speech he repeated several times during the 1988 election campaign. When he came to the section on taxes, he used to say: "Read . . . my . . . lips [the *link*, very deliberately spoken] . . . no . . . new . . . taxes" [the message he wished to get over].

The rhetorical question needs little explanation. "Where do we go from here?" and "How far can we take this conclusion?" are typical examples and it is not difficult to devise a ready supply when preparing a presentation. A danger to beware of is that rhetorical questions can sound pompous if overdone or put in the wrong place. At worst, it can prompt some comedian in the audience to volunteer a silly answer, although this might not necessarily be disadvantageous, as will be seen when interruptions are discussed.

Repetition

Budding presenters can learn a great deal about repetition from politicians, schoolteachers and advertising executives, who know that most messages, especially those which embody an unfamiliar idea, are not automatically absorbed the first time round. They sometimes go to extreme lengths of repetition, arguing that tedium does not matter as long as the message sticks.

Excess of this kind is hardly likely to go down well with a business audience but, used with discretion, repetition is a useful aid to promoting understanding, especially when combined with pausing.

There is no surer way of bringing home some salient point, understanding of which is vital to the argument, than to pause, then repeat it, preferable in slightly different words. Repetition serves a similar purpose to a visual aid, in that both invite the audience to take particular note of the point being made. In practice these steps can effectively follow in sequence, like this:

(a) make the point — pause —
(b) show the visual aid — pause —
(c) repeat the point.

Summarising

Summarising combines the characteristics of pausing and repetition and is appropriate at stages throughout a presentation. It enables the audience to catch its breath and the presenter to recapitulate what has been said so far. Summarising is also the only satisfactory (and, to the audience, quite inconspicuous) solution if a presenter has lost the thread or suffered a mishap of any other kind.

Pausing, repetition and summarising all have the affect of slowing down a presenter's delivery (and therefore contributing to variation of pace), which is desirable in itself, particularly in the case of naturally fluent and fast speakers.

Look for Models

There are many good models around and a great deal can be learned by listening to and observing professionals, bad points as well as good. For those who know what to look for, it is an excellent method of self-improvement to notice what it is that public performers do to project themselves effectively or, on the other hand, what may be spoiling their performance. Those who give a fair number of presentations find they do this unconsciously and make a mental note of what to do or not to do when next they perform.

Intelligibility and interest are vital ingredients of a successful presentation. The most fascinating text is unlikely to achieve its purpose if its delivery is so boring and obscure that nobody can or wishes to understand it. Time devoted to understanding and improving use of the devices which assist effective delivery is, therefore, well spent.

Interruptions

All presenters sooner or later have to deal with interruptions, whether from an internal or external source. External noises off are a nuisance because they often cannot be controlled. Fortunately, most of them do not last long. Of course, if they persist something has to be done (although preferably not by the presenter). The golden rule is not to try to compete with them. The main problem is discontinuity: there will be some loss of contact with the audience which will have to be regained when things have settled down again. This is all the more difficult if presenters have allowed themselves to get impatient. It is necessary to retain good humour and keep as much in touch with the audience as possible. Then, when they are ready to resume, they can summarise what has been said so far and carry on.

Internal interruptions are a different matter, as the presenter can usually retain control and may well be able to turn the situation to advantage. In most circumstances the majority of members of the audience are there to listen and are unlikely to be sympathetic to a minority, still less a single individual, trying to prevent them doing so. The bulk of the audience is therefore sympathetic to the presenter rather than to the interrupter.

It is important to deal with an interruption positively and good humouredly. It may have taken the form of a question or a comment, possibly a criticism, even a disparagement. Whatever its form, it should be treated seriously, like any question or comment in the normal way. Presenters should try, if they can, to give the impression that the interruption is not unwelcome, in that it enables them to make a point they were coming to anyway. If the interruption is clearly frivolous (like a gratuitous response to a rhetorical question), it should be dealt with in the same spirit: as a welcome diversion amid serious proceedings. The point to remember is that annoyance on the presenter's part will be counter-productive, whereas an amiable reaction can only be beneficial.

Inattention

Absolute attention from an audience is so rare that it can be discounted. However interesting in content and delivery, all presentations go through one or more low patches somewhere or other. When this happens it is clearly important to get things moving again as quickly as possible.

The antidote to inattention is to arouse the audience by means of a change of tempo or direction. Just as a sleeper is unaffected by a steady noise, but wakes up when it stops, so the audience will take notice if the presenter does something different. Something as simple as a visual aid, a movement of some kind or raising the pitch of the voice (variation of pitch and pace) can get things moving again. If more is needed, a relevant anecdote or illustration (perhaps from the stock all presenters should have in reserve) or an interim summary can usually do the trick. Whatever it is, the presenter must do *something* — inattention is a condition that can spread.

The odd person in the audience who is inattentive can be discounted. There is usually someone who feels that there is something more useful to be done than listen to the presenter. And again, some people can seem inattentive, but be listening closely. It is only where there is inattention on the part of a significant number of the audience that action is needed.

On the other hand, if there is a group that starts chattering or making signals to each other, no time should be lost in nipping it in the bud. A proven method is to pause, look at the offenders and wait (it will not be a long wait) until they return to the fold; meanwhile, the remainder of the audience will be on the side of the presenter. The presentation can then continue, as after any other interruption.

The one thing an interrupted presenter should never do is to plead with the audience: anything of the "Come on, ladies and gentlemen, you may benefit from what I have to say" variety will inevitably result in embarrassment and distancing.

Time

Awareness of time is an essential attribute in a presenter. Business presentations in particular should start and finish on time. Starting on time is sometimes out of the hands of the presenter, but to overrun is a bad habit and to avoid this the presenter must not lose track of the passage of time; this is where a guide time at intervals in notes can be invaluable.

The amount of time expended in any event is its duration multiplied by the number of people present. In a business context time is an expensive commodity. People in business do not listen to presentations for amusement or diversion. They do it because it is part of their job. They have many things to attend to and this means that not only their time but also their attention span is limited. The presenter should always carry a watch: not all rooms have a clock and clocks are sometimes inaccurate or out of sight.

In practice, presentations seldom run perfectly to schedule, but the solution is simple. Presenters who overrun should speed up or omit some of the non-essential material. If they underrun, some reserve material can be brought in — preferably an anecdote or illustration. Question time (see Chapter 8) is a useful refuge if there is either overrunning or underrunning. If the former, questions might have to be curtailed (although always reluctantly); if the latter, they can be invited earlier than intended. And remember that few audiences find it unacceptable to finish a little early.

Awareness of the Audience

Awareness of the audience remains central to successful delivery and it sometimes does a presenter good to be interrupted in order to be reminded that the audience are still there.

Awareness enables a presenter to sense an audience's mood and reaction: whether they are attentive; whether they can hear; or have had enough dry facts for the time being and deserve some diversion. The great advantage of speaking from notes is that it is possible to make adjustments and this slight element of uncertainty can help to make a presentation seem fresh and natural.

Preparation and awareness of the audience are, in fact, the only real essentials in delivering a successful presentation. The devices suggested in this chapter are valuable and worth perfecting, but they are skills that come almost unconsciously to presenters who have prepared well and are in tune with the audience.

Ending

Bringing the proceedings to a close logically, decisively and gracefully is by no means the easiest part of a presentation. There is a natural tendency as the end approaches to wish to escape as quickly as possible.

However pressing their wish to escape, presenters should aim to deliver their final passage (prepared beforehand and memorised, of course) with authority and on an up beat and, having done that, to maintain contact with the audience a little *beyond* the end. It is necessary only to remain still for a few seconds. In many an otherwise good presentation the only signal of finality is a rather limp "thank you for listening to me". To be able to end positively is an attribute well worth cultivating.

Applause, if any, should be accepted graciously and with evident pleasure. An appreciative audience deserves nothing less.

Summary

(a) A good script can be spoiled by poor delivery.
(b) Maintaining rapport with the audience is a continuous responsibility.
(c) Presenters should look their best, move unhurriedly and act with authority.
(d) Any physical barriers between presenter and audience should, if possible, be removed.
(e) Presenters should not start until they have attention.
(f) Most people can reach an acceptable standard of delivery, if they know how, but they must be prepared to practise hard.
(g) Intelligibility is assisted by paragraphing, signposting and emphasis.
(h) The devices used to promote both intelligibility and interest are variation of pitch and pace, pausing, the use of linking phrases and rhetorical questions, repetition, and intermittent summarising.
(i) Do not try to compete with external interruptions and handle interruptions from the audience with good humour and patience.
(j) Inattention is best relieved by a change of tempo or direction.
(k) If there is loss of continuity, the best way to get back on stream is an interim summary.
(l) Keep an eye on the time and adjust as necessary.
(m) Close on an up beat and do not hurry away.

Chapter 7
Good and Bad Habits

This chapter deals with humour, audibility, gesture and movement, and mannerisms. Good habits in these can enhance, and bad habits detract from, the delivery of the presentation.

Humour

Any presentation is better for a bit of humour: an amiable manner, a pleasantry, a story — all these help to warm the atmosphere and the relationship between presenter and audience. It is necessary to distinguish, however, between good humour, in the sense of cheerfulness and a wish to please, and humour intended to raise a laugh.

Lack of good humour is detrimental, however serious the purpose of the presentation. A heavy, unsmiling manner tends to make an audience unsympathetic and the task of the presenter more difficult. Not many speakers are so eloquent and persuasive that complete seriousness is no handicap — Enoch Powell is perhaps one of the few. An easy atmosphere between presenter and audience is a lubricant which helps the former to relax and the latter to be more receptive. It has a reciprocal quality, a happy mood on one side encouraging and feeding off a happy mood on the other. Like many other good qualities, however, it is possible to go too far. Unfailing good cheer, when gravity would be more appropriate, becomes tedious and worst of all is a cheeky "all pals together" manner (often a cloak for nervousness). It must not be forgotten that business presentations more often than not have a serious purpose. This does not mean they have to be gloomy occasions, but hearty jokiness is usually out of place.

So the aim should be a sensible middle course, cheerful and pleasant, but with an overall sense of the purpose of the occasion.

Humour in the sense of amusement is another thing and business presentations are quite different from, for example, after dinner speeches, whose specific purpose is enjoyment and relaxation and where a succession of jokes is expected.

In a business presentation jokes as such should be attempted only cautiously. If they are witty and well told, they may be acceptable, but not many presenters have this facility. The first rule about jokes is that presenters who are not reasonably expert raconteurs should do without them.

Even when told well, too many jokes are usually a distraction. The second rule, then, is to be sparing with jokes.

The third rule is that they should be (or can be told in such a way that they appear to be) relevant, so that they emerge naturally within the mainstream of the text.

The most reliable form of humour in a business presentation is usually no more than a relevant one liner, especially if it is spontaneous. Presenters may by all means have some humorous material prepared, but should hold it back until they sense that the timing and mood of the audience are right. Much humour occurring in presentations is, in fact, unplanned and even unconscious. Presenters often get a laugh and may be quite unaware what has prompted it — but it is a sweet sound, whatever the cause.

Light hearted anecdotes which bear on the subject matter need only be mildly funny to be well received. And a small amount of poetic licence in telling the story is perfectly permissible. But the pudding should not be over egged; too many one liners can be as tedious as too many jokes.

Attempts at humour quite often fall flat. There is only one thing to do: move on as quickly and calmly as possible. The audience is more than likely not to notice anything; but any discomposure on the part of the presenter is almost certain to be noticed. Rejoinders such as "That was supposed to be funny" go down as badly as "I am now going to tell you a joke".

The final rule is that, if the slightest doubt crosses a presenter's mind about whether to use a particular joke, the answer is "no". Jokes in a presentation are too risky to take chances with.

Audibility

If the audience cannot hear or make out what is being said, the presenter is wasting everyone's time, as well as all the time spent in preparation. Audiences will strain their ears for a time, but sooner or later they will switch off and the presenter might as well be addressing an empty room.

Some people are endowed with a voice that carries naturally. If they also enunciate their words clearly, their listeners will have no problems. Naturally slow speakers tend to have the edge in this respect. It is important for presenters to make themselves aware of how they speak, so that they can as far as possible correct their shortcomings.

In speech there are good habits, which have to be cultivated, and bad habits, which have to be avoided.

Good Habits

Speech results when (a) air from the lungs is expired past the vocal chords, (b) the vocal chords vibrate, creating sound, (c) the sound is shaped by the teeth, tongue and lips, and (d) the sound resonates within the chest, throat and nasal cavities before emerging from the mouth.

To enable the voice to perform as well as possible, presenters have to do everything they can to enable these physical processes to function properly. Correct breathing is the basis of clear enunciation, but unfortunately the circumstances of making a presentation tend to magnify any breathing deficiencies. The delivery needs to be given plenty of air and the following suggestions may help.

(a) Give the lungs and cavities a fair chance by standing up straight, with head, neck and shoulders relaxed. To contort the body or lean forward (as over a lectern or table) has an adverse effect.
(b) Get into the habit of breathing deeply into the base of the lungs and breathing out slowly and evenly. This is related to the suggestion about relaxation in Chapter 1.
(c) Give full value to each syllable. This often means speaking more slowly than usual.
(d) Speak out — shouting is unnecessary — and aim the voice towards the back of the room, so that it covers the whole of the audience. It is necessary to make a conscious effort to *let* the voice resonate, rather than *make* it resonate. The way to do this is to pitch the voice

higher than customary, as though singing. The result will be to bring the nasal, rather than the chest and throat, cavities (the "resonators") into play, thus giving the voice a sharper timbre, which tends to carry better.

Cultivation of good habits will go a long way towards preventing bad ones, of which a presenter must, however, be aware, in order to control them.

Bad Habits

The following are the faults that seem to be most frequently encountered. The remedies suggested are fairly obvious, although that is not to say they are easy to put into practice. But with perseverence they seem to work.

(a) *Speaking softly* is an often encountered fault, resulting sometimes from shyness as much as a naturally quiet voice. The antidote is to make an effort to open out the lungs and aim at the back row.
(b) *Speaking from the back of the throat* is a fault to which people with deep voices are particularly prone: men are worse than women in this respect. The remedy is to make a conscious effort to speak out and raise the pitch of the voice.
(c) *Muttering* is theoretically easy to cure, as the antidote is simply to move the lips more positively. It is helpful if presenters imagine that the audience have to read their lips.
(d) *Running syllables together* is a common fault, found in many dialect speakers and also among quite fluent (perhaps too fluent) speakers. It may be acceptable in conversation between those whose ears are attuned to it, but before an audience it has a serious effect on audibility. The cure is to articulate more deliberately.
(e) *Garbled and mispronounced consonants* result partly from carelessness and partly, in some cases, from inadequate control of the muscles of the tongue and lips. It can be controlled by more deliberate articulation, achievable by some only after a great deal of practice. Practice is in fact a necessary chore for all those with bad voice habits, who wish to make a comprehensible speech.
(f) *Failure to speak directly to the audience* results from failure to *look* at the audience: the two things go together.

(g) *Tailing off* is a common failing, even among those who articulate well, and consists in dropping the voice, usually at the end, but sometimes in the middle, of a phrase or sentence. One reason may be a compulsion to get to the end of a passage; another may be shortage of breath (which is correctable); but a more usual cause seems to be that people making a presentation or a speech tend to think ahead to what they are going to say next and in doing so get careless about what they are currently saying. The tendency to tail off can be greatly reduced and even eliminated by means of those indispensable components of good delivery: a deliberate pace, pauses at key intervals, and appropriate emphasis. All these also go a long way to preventing many of the other bad habits mentioned.

Microphones

No discussion of audibility would be complete without mentioning the subject of artificial aids. This does not arise in most business circumstances, where, even if the necessary equipment is available, it is often not worth the trouble to set it up.

Presenters who have a microphone at hand and doubt whether their voice will carry should not hesitate to use it. But remember that a microphone on a stand makes for immobility and one in the hand leaves the speaker essentially one handed. A neck microphone is best, but be careful not to trip over any cable. As with any other equipment, check beforehand that it works.

One other thing has to be said, however. A microphone merely *amplifies* the voice; it does not correct its shortcomings. In fact, it amplifies bad habits as well as good. Use of a microphone, therefore, in no sense makes it unnecessary to cultivate good diction.

The Speaker of the House of Commons was asked by a member whether the microphones could be turned up, as he could not hear the speeches because of background interruptions. The Speaker declined, pointing out that to do so would also increase the volume of the interruptions.

Voice Improvement

The subject of self-improvement in general is dealt with in Chapter 9, but one feature of voice improvement should be mentioned here. Diction is an area where would-be improvers are particularly self-conscious. Many appear to be inhibited about modifying their accustomed manner of speaking. Perhaps they think the practices of a lifetime are unalterable, although, while some find it harder than others, few people are constitutionally unable to adopt the good habits and avoid the bad ones listed. They may also believe they will sound different or seem to be putting on airs and graces.

Such doubters may be assured that their accent and style of speech need not change (although accents *can* be modified if, but only if, that is the wish of the individual). Their voices will sound as before and their friends will have no difficulty in recognising them. The only change, and that must surely be for the better, is that they will speak more clearly and their voices will carry better.

Presenters who wish to improve their enunciation have to throw off their inhibitions and have a go, bearing in mind that all their careful preparations will be wasted if the audience fails to hear or understand what they are saying.

Gesture and Movement

Effective presentation can be greatly enhanced by appropriate gestures and movement, which are also important elements in maintaining contact with the audience. They have the additional value of slowing down the rate of speech and relaxing the body. But both can be overdone to the point where they are embarrassingly exaggerated or degenerate into fidgeting. To avoid these dangers presenters must ensure that their gestures and movements are consistent with their words. For example: to emphasise something small, raise a hand and open the fingers; to indicate distance, open out the arms; when talking about generosity, open the hands. The open hand, palm up, is more reassuring than the clenched hand, palm down; the relaxed gesture is less distracting than the abrupt. Gesture, within reasonable bounds, has another use, in that it opens out a presenter's stance and reduces the common tendency to adopt a defensive, crossed hands posture.

Gestures should be employed confidently, but also with discretion. The sweep of the arms, the clenched fist, the stabbing finger, beloved of politicians and trade union leaders, may be acceptable in their place, but are not appropriate in a business environment. Another practice to avoid is the incessant gesturing to which many "media" people are prone when they appear on television; every syllable, it seems, has to be accompanied by a sharp movement of the hand.

Head and eye (including eyebrow) gestures are a most effective means of giving emphasis to words and animation to the face. They also have the happy by-product of cementing a sympathetic bond with the audience. This is a field where the better television presenters provide excellent models.

Here again, however, beware of excess: nothing is more tiresome than a perpetually nodding head. Head and eye gestures, like those of hand and arm, should be purposeful and in harmony with the words.

The design of many lecture rooms makes *movement*, as distinct from gesture, difficult. It is not feasible to move to any significant extent behind a table or lectern (which sometimes cannot be avoided). Many people, too, object to a presenter moving about, on the ground that it diverts attention from the words and it is true that *excessive* movement is a distraction and can be an annoyance. Some movement does, however, help a presenter to relax and, in giving the audience a fresh viewpoint, reduces the possibility of monotony. But this must be said with the important proviso that the movement should be purposeful. Walking across to use or point out something on a visual aid is a good example of purposeful movement. A less obvious example is when a presenter takes a step or two towards the audience to emphasise some important point (or wake it up if attention is flagging!).

Above all, gestures and movements should be those which come easily to the individual. They must appear natural and not forced; comfortable for both presenter and audience. Arriving at the appropriate balance must be a matter of trial and error.

Mannerisms

Certain bad habits regarding enunciation, visual aids, gesture and movement have already been covered. This section deals with habits which in a general sense distract attention from what is being said.

It has already been noted that 100 per cent attention is virtually impossible to achieve, even when an audience is intensely interested in the subject matter. A presenter has to work hard in various ways to maximise attention and to ensure that it is particularly directed to the more significant points.

The level of attention also varies between different members of the audience, some of whom all too readily latch on to a distraction, in order to have a rest from listening.

Mannerisms are detrimental to a presentation, not because they are necessarily harmful in themselves, but because they distract the attention of the audience from what presenters are saying to what they are *doing*. A mannerism which may be trivial in itself, unnoticed or immediately forgotten if done only once, has a hypnotic effect if continuously repeated. Instead of attending to the words, the audience tend to concentrate on the possibility of it occurring again and the more often it occurs, the greater will be the fascination. It would be possible to give an almost endless recital of mannerisms and the following examples are by no means exhaustive.

(a) *Fidgeting* can involve foot tapping, compulsive touching of the face or body, or fiddling with a piece of jewellery. An object in the hand, such as a pointer or felt pen, that is not currently in use, is liable to be fiddled with. Notes can be another temptation: presenters should move them as an extension of the body, but when the body is still, the notes should be kept still.

(b) *Addictions*, such as repeatedly clearing the throat, humming, hawing, or pursing the lips, can be particularly distracting.

(c) *A hand in the pocket* (mostly men) usually results in remembering after a while that it is there and taking it out. Then in it goes again and so forth. It is not long before the audience starts to anticipate the in and out movement.

(d) *Word repetition* is something nearly everyone indulges in to some extent in ordinary conversation. There are endless possibilities, such as "you know," "sort of," "actually," "I mean," and "basically". Presenters should make an effort to keep any such habit in check as it poses the same hazards as any other form of repetition.

Since mannerisms that are over-indulged run the risk of becoming bad habits, presenters should get into the *good* habit of watching out for them. It is useful to have one or two "candid colleagues" (whose value will be mentioned in Chapter 9) to act as monitors.

Summary

Humour

(a) A pleasant manner is always an asset in a presenter.
(b) Well timed humour, if not excessive, enlivens a presentation.
(c) Jokes should be relevant and attempted only if the presenter can tell them well.
(d) Topical one liners are the most reliable form of humour.
(e) Move on quickly if an attempt at humour misfires.

Audibility

(f) A presentation that cannot be heard or understood is a waste of time.
(g) It is good to
 (i) stand up straight
 (ii) breathe properly
 (iii) articulate each syllable
 (iv) speak out.
(h) It is bad to
 (i) speak too softly
 (ii) speak from the back of the throat
 (iii) mutter
 (iv) run syllables together
 (v) garble consonants
 (vi) fail to project towards the audience
 (vii) tail off.
(i) Deliberate delivery, pausing and emphasis can reduce speech faults.
(j) Microphones are useful, but they amplify good and bad points alike.
(k) To improve diction, it is necessary for presenters to practise and discard any inhibitions about modifying their accustomed manner of speech.

Gesture and Movement

(l) Appropriate gesture and movement add to the effectiveness of a presentation, are a good means of emphasis, and enhance rapport with the audience.

(m) Both should be done purposefully and confidently, but neither to excess.

Mannerisms

(n) Repeated mannerisms distract attention, because they have a hypnotic tendency.

(o) Self-correction is valuable but difficult and it is helpful to have a candid colleague to point out any mannerisms that should be avoided.

Chapter 8
Questions

It used to be told of Field Marshal Viscount Montgomery that at the end of a speech he would announce, "There will be no questions: I have made myself perfectly clear". If that were a general philosophy, this chapter would be superfluous, but in a business presentation, at any rate, an opportunity for questions is expected.

The term "questions" should be taken to embrace also comments and criticisms and the term "answers" to cover any response by the presenter. The best practice at the appropriate time is to invite the audience to offer "comments or questions", thus indicating that "question time" is as much an opportunity for audience participation as for further contributions from the presenter.

The value of question time to the presenter is that the audience can indicate the ground they are interested in, as well as any gaps in the presentation they would like covered. The rapport the presenter has striven to establish can thus be cemented.

Question time is, however, by its nature, unstructured and unpredictable. It has to be handled with skill and confidence so that it does not get out of control and away from the subject. Valuable as audience participation may be, the basic purpose of a presentation is to examine a particular theme and not indulge in free for all discussion.

During preparation, therefore, presenters have to give a good deal of thought to the way they intend to handle questions and make up their minds, first, how much time is to be allocated to questions and, second, at what point (or points) in the proceedings to invite them.

There cannot be a definitive rule about the proportion of the total time available that should be devoted to questions, since circumstances are infinitely variable. Nevertheless, it is useful to have a yardstick against which to determine the appropriate balance between presentation and questions in any given situation.

An extreme position, occasionally held, is that as little time as possible should be allowed for questions. The more common view is that 25 per cent of the total time is about right, but many experienced presenters favour even more, sometimes up to 50 per cent. There are, of course, occasions where it is appropriate, perhaps inevitable, that there be no questions at all. For example, how much time can be given to questions when the total time available is ten minutes?

The reasons for allowing more, rather than less, time for questions in a business presentation are as follows:

(a) A business audience expect to have an adequate opportunity to test the presenter's views. Indeed, one measure of the effectiveness of a presentation is the number of questions that come up.
(b) An audience's attention span is limited. Curtailing presentation time, in order to allow more questions, reduces any tendency towards overloading.
(c) Similarly, the longer the presentation goes on, the greater is the chance of the audience getting bored. It is tempting fate to hold the floor for too long.
(d) Making a presentation generates nervous tension. Question time, if approached positively, can be a welcome relief to a presenter in that the audience has then to do some of the work.
(e) Question time provides an opportunity to insert any important points that may have been missed. It is often possible to get these in quite naturally as part of a reply to a question; otherwise it is perfectly permissible to volunteer a missing item.
(f) For practical purposes, it is useful to have a reserve of time available. Presentations seldom go precisely to schedule and, if generous time has been allowed for questions, it provides a cushion against overrunning.

The main arguments put forward for keeping question time short, on the other hand, are that:

(a) presenters then retain maximum control
(b) they may not know the answers
(c) they may be left stranded for lack of questions

(d) making a presentation is ordeal enough without the additional burden of questions.

A more constructive view, however, is that question time is not just a matter of knowing the answers, but also an opportunity for discussion of the chosen subject with a group of people whose interest the presenter has succeeded in arousing.

When to Take Questions

The second decision to be made is at what point in the proceedings questions should be invited. The usual, and on the whole most satisfactory, place is at the end, an arrangement which enables presenters to manage time more easily and adhere to their prepared framework. In the case of a presentation that is read word for word, there is, of course, no choice but to take questions at the end.

Where the subject matter is complex and the audience are likely to be particularly interested, a useful variant is to take questions after each section. Interim questions are rather time consuming and need to be firmly controlled, but are an excellent arrangement in the right circumstances.

A third possibility is to allow members of the audience to raise questions and comments whenever they wish. If this goes well, there need be no fears about inattention or lack of interest. This pattern makes great demands on the presenter in that control of time and subject matter can easily slip away and, however satisfied the audience may be, some of the more important material may not be adequately covered.

To deal effectively with random questioning, it is necessary, therefore, to:

(a) deflect irrelevant, and curtail over-long, contributions
(b) be a good judge of pace so that each phase gets its due share of time
(c) be prepared to juggle different parts of the script, if necessary changing the planned sequence
(d) firmly classify the essential and non-essential points in case some of the material has to be dropped.

Confidently handled, random questions can be highly satisfying and enjoyable both for presenter and audience. Ideally, the audience should:

(a) be reasonably familiar with the subject matter or at least able to grasp the drift without difficulty and
(b) be of manageable size — 15 people is about the maximum.

It must be borne in mind, however, that in business situations, especially where senior colleagues or potentially big customers are involved, there is sometimes no choice but to take questions as they come. It is not always easy with this kind of audience to persuade its members to preserve their questions until *the presenter* is ready to receive them. It is wise, therefore, to try to anticipate this situation and consider how to handle it if it arises.

Whatever the circumstances, control of the proceedings will always be better if presenters announce at the beginning how they intend to take questions. The audience will then know where they stand and, although some of them may not always be able to contain themselves, most of them will usually go along with the presenter's wishes.

How then should questions (using the term in a wide sense to include comments and criticisms) be approached?

Preparation

As for every other aspect of a presentation, preparation for questions is vital. Presenters should try to forecast what the questions will be and how they will answer them. It is useful to find out if there is likely to be anyone in the audience with special interests who may raise some less familiar point.

Thought should also be given to possible awkward, perhaps irrelevant, questions and the best way of dealing with them. Will it be better to give an honest answer or to try to turn the question back on the questioner? If the latter, it is important always to be diplomatic, for taking a rise out of one of the audience is a certain way of forfeiting sympathy, however provocative he or she may have been.

A great deal of help in preparing for questions can come from immediate colleagues, who are useful as a sounding board to judge the effectiveness of the proposed answers and whether they are likely to lead to difficult supplementary questions.

Another useful precaution during preparation is to "plant" potential questions in the script — for example "I can deal with this in more detail, if you wish, during question time".

Silence

Many budding presenters are worried that, having invited questions, they may be met with an apparently stubborn silence. How should this be dealt with?

As with most problems, prevention is better than cure. Some of the reasons for an audience's hestitation are shyness, unwillingness to be the first to speak or fear that the question may appear stupid. Audiences, like presenters, tend to suffer from nerves at the prospect of coming in cold.

But the audience have the advantage that a mentor is available, in the shape of the presenter, to dispel any nerves. It follows that the presenter who has cultivated a warm rapport with the audience is far more likely to stimulate questions than one who is felt to be remote. Equally, the more interesting and comprehensible the content of the presentation the more readily will questions be prompted.

Two other things can be done by way of prevention. One has already been suggested: to "plant" a potential question by leaving a loose end in the body of the presentation. The second device is to prime an acquaintance in the audience with one or more questions to feed in if there is a hiatus; but to do it only on a signal, as otherwise there is a danger of interrupting a spontaneous question about to emerge.

However well the ground has been prepared, there may still be an initial silence. Presenters should not be put off by this: their demeanour is all important. If they give the impression that they do not *expect* questions, the audience may easily infer that they do not *want* questions. It is important to look expectant, as though it were a matter of course that the audience should have questions. Presenters should maintain eye contact and dwell encouragingly on anyone who seems to be waiting for the ice to break.

> There is a warning in the example of one presenter, experienced enough to know better, who, having invited questions, then looked away and started to pack his papers, as though eager to depart — which he soon did, in the absence of any response at all from the audience!

If the audience continue to be unresponsive, there are still a number of things that can be done, such as the following (but it is necessary to be patient and not rush into them):

(a) The presenter can pick on an individual, especially one who can be identified by name and is known to have a particular interest.
(b) The presenter can give a signal (clear and agreed beforehand) to a primed questioner.
(c) The presenter can use a phrase such as "I thought someone might wish to ask me about. . .". A variant of this is to bring out some non-essential point or (even better) an anecdote from reserve material.

Presenters should also be ready to use any of the above stratagems, again not too eagerly, if there is a lull in questioning. But if the subject and presentation have been at all interesting, once the questions start the problem is likely to be how to halt them (of which more shortly).

However, it is inevitable there will be the odd occasion when the flow of questions is sluggish. If it is clear that questions have dried up (or there have been none at all) the proceedings should be brought politely to an end.

Do not lose confidence if this happens, as the reason for the lack of questions may well be something entirely unconnected with the quality of the presentation or the interest aroused. In the business world, attending a presentation is likely to be only one of many things of concern to members of the audience and sometimes they may have good reason to wish to get away as quickly as possible.

For example, a consultant was reporting back on a market research assignment. To her astonishment, for it was an important project, there were no questions and the audience dispersed rapidly. Only later did she learn that a takeover bid had been made for the company and everyone was eager to find out what was happening.

Answering a Question

It is unwise of presenters to attempt to answer a question they do not fully understand; if in doubt they should check with the questioner that they have got it right. They should then repeat the question, paraphrased or simplified, if necessary, for the benefit of the rest of the audience. This is an important precaution, as questions are not always audible or well framed. If there is a roving microphone, it is still wise to repeat the question, which, although it may have been heard, may not necessarily have been understood by everyone.

The one basic rule about answering a question is to answer it directly. It is true that questions are sometimes convoluted or based on a false premise or assume a knowledge which others in the audience may not possess. There is a temptation in such circumstances to preface the answer with some explanatory background, in order to place it in an accurate context, but it is better not to do so. To fail to get to the point of a question straight away is, in the first place, time consuming; secondly, it can give an impression, however unjustified, of hedging; and, thirdly, presenters may get so involved in explaining the background that they forget the gist of the question.

When asked a question, answer it without qualifications and only then, if necessary, add any supplementary explanation.

There is a second equally important rule: answer as briefly as possible. The fact that brevity is not always easy when the presenter is taken by surprise underlines the value of forecasting and framing answers to potential questions during preparation. Whether anticipated or not, however, questions should be taken slowly and calmly and presenters might remember that they can gain a little time when they repeat the substance of the question before starting to answer it.

This is not to imply that all answers have to be short and snappy. It is a matter of judging what is reasonable, balancing the requirements of the current question with the need to preserve sufficient time for other questions. Most presenters find, as they gain experience of question time, that they are able to judge the right length and content of their answers almost instinctively.

It is legitimate for presenters to slip in something important that they have omitted to include in the main presentation. This may be done either in the course of answering a question which covers reasonably similar ground or by offering the additional point as a separate contribution, for example: "I forgot to mention. . .".

What is *not* permissible, however, is to encroach unduly on question time with what amounts effectively to a resumption of the presentation.

Snags

Presenters are bound to encounter snags now and then during question time. Audiences do not expect them to be perfect and will think none the worse of them if they are occasionally stumped. What does cause problems, however, is when presenters draw attention to any difficulty by becoming flustered or being over-apologetic or, worse still, trying to bluff their way through. This is another example where a stumble is usually overlooked and often not noticed, but making a fuss about it creates unnecessary embarrassment.

Presenters should not be afraid of the occasional piece of repartee, delivered with a light touch, of course, but must move on quickly if it falls flat.

A sales executive fielded an awkward question and also got a laugh with the words: "See me afterwards"; the ambiguity of her retort gained piquancy from the fact that she was extremely attractive.

It may be helpful to mention some of the commoner snags that can occur and suggest what can be done about them.

(a) The circumstance that most alarms inexperienced presenters is the question to which they do not know the answer. Do not hesitate, if possible, to deflect the question to a colleague in the audience who is better informed on the point. Failing that, throw it to the audience at large. Remember that question time is an opportunity for give and take and not just a session as from teacher to pupils. In the last resort, undertake to find out the answer as soon as possible (and, of course, do not neglect to do so). It is, incidentally, sometimes fairly obvious that the questioner in fact knows the answer and is simply testing the presenter. The best way of tackling this is to admit ignorance, invite the questioner to supply the information and offer thanks for the assistance.

On one occasion an engineer was supplied by this means with the answer to a practical problem that had eluded him for weeks. His admission of this went down well with the audience.

(b) A snag that may call for delicate handling is the specialised question which is of limited interest to most of the audience. An erudite discussion between the presenter and a few others can be frustrating for the excluded majority. The best course is to thank the questioner for the contribution, comment on it briefly and offer to pursue it privately afterwards.
(c) It may be that an adequate answer to a question would take a disproportionate length of time. Whether or not it is dealt with there and then depends on the amount of general interest in the topic and how much time is available. If interest is likely to be limited, it may be better to acknowledge it politely and offer to pursue it later.
(d) A member of the audience who has difficulty in framing a question deserves tactful assistance in putting the right words together. Presenters who provide this help, without drawing undue attention to the limitations of the individual, earn the person's gratitude, impress the rest of the audience with their sensitivity and perhaps persuade some other reticent questioner that there need be no embarrassment in speaking up.
(e) It is necessary to be firm with questions that are inordinately lengthy, sometimes amounting to a mini speech. A proven method of handling this is to concentrate on what is being said and, having grasped the gist of the question, to jump in as soon as reasonable: it is essential to move fast. The presenter should than paraphrase the question and answer it politely.
(f) A deliberately provocative, and often irrelevant, question should be answered as though it were intended as a serious contribution, but without spending undue time on it. The audience as a whole is likely to be grateful for the offender being despatched as unceremoniously, but politely, as possible.

Closure

The clock is as important during questions as during the presentation. Question time has to be paced, so that as many as possible of those who wish to contribute get a fair opportunity to do so. Presenters therefore have to be alert and sensitive, as well as firm, where necessary. As the end approaches, sufficient time should be allowed for the final question and also for a concluding contribution from the presenter. These final few sentences should encapsulate the general drift of the presentation, substantially prepared beforehand, but subject to amendment in the light of any particularly significant questions.

A few minutes from the end, invite "one quick final question". Do not wait too long for it. If a question comes, answer it briefly; if not, move decisively to the concluding remarks. Then sit down and make it clear that the session is over.

Presenters may sometimes be pressed, if things are going well, to extend questions beyond the allotted time. If there are further presentations to follow or any other constraint on continuing, they have no choice but to decline, but, if there is no obvious reason to the contrary, they may be tempted to carry on. It is flattering and comforting to be in this position, especially if they approached the presentation with a certain amount of trepidation and may feel they owe a debt to the audience.

However strong their inclination to continue, it is better for presenters to end at the appointed time and not go beyond the period for which they have paced themselves. The dividing line between too little and too much is a thin one and, if they have reached the end on a high note, they would be unwise to push their luck further. Another reason for ending on time is that for all those in the audience who wish to continue with questions, there will be at least as many who have other things to do. As for those who have, or claim to have, more questions, they could be invited to have an informal session afterwards. If, of course, the pressure to continue is from a senior colleague or a potentially lucrative customer or sponsor, business requirements must take precedence.

The Chair

Occupants of the chair, if any, who insist on controlling question time can be an embarrassment. Those who are discreet will have withdrawn from the front, to return only when the proceedings are about to be wound up or time is running out. In the case of those who are inclined otherwise it is worthwhile trying politely to persuade them to allow question time to be run in the way the presenter wishes. Of course, if the person in the chair is determined to enjoy a bit of the limelight, there is no choice but to accede gracefully.

Summary

(a) Make it clear to the audience that "questions" includes comments, criticisms and any other points for discussion.
(b) As question time is essentially unstructured, it has to be controlled and thoroughly prepared. Try to predict likely questions and how to answer them.
(c) Decide beforehand how much time to devote to questions (with a bias towards generosity) and at what point questions may be taken. Inform the audience accordingly.
(d) Do not rely on an instant flow of questions and help the audience to overcome any initial hesitation. Prepare for a possible shortage of questions by "planting" potential questions in the presentation and priming one or more colleagues with "reserve" questions.
(e) Before answering a question, make sure its meaning is clear and repeat it for the benefit of the audience.
(f) Answer the question directly before adding any supplementary explanation. Be brief, although it is permissible, if appropriate, to work in any relevant material that has been overlooked.
(g) If a presenter does not know the answer, the question should, if possible, be deflected to someone better informed in the audience. The alternative is to undertake to find out the answer.
(h) If a question is of limited interest or an adequate answer would take too long, tactfully suggest dealing with it privately later.
(i) Be patient with ponderous or hesitant questions; tactfully curtail over-long questions; and deal firmly with deliberately awkward questions.
(j) Close punctually and decisively, allowing sufficient time for a final summing up. Resist any plea for an extension of question time.
(k) Try to dissuade the occupant of the chair, if any, from taking over question time.

Chapter 9
Rehearsal

Rehearsal is an intrinsic part of preparation, but it could not be dealt with until the chapters on delivery and related matters had been completed.

The process of rehearsal actually starts with the decision to make a presentation, although at that stage the presenter may have only a vague idea of its form and substance. Rehearsal continues as the presentation is committed to paper, because presenters tend to visualise what they are writing in the form of the spoken word. As it is an automatic, partly subconscious, action, however, it tends to be uncoordinated and is therefore of limited value. For rehearsal to be effective, it has to be put on a systematic footing. This indeed is the whole essence of a successful business presentation: that every aspect is approached in a businesslike way.

When presenters contemplate rehearsal, they must put aside any illusions that it is painless. It is, for one thing, time consuming and, if it is to be worthwhile, there is the additional consideration that changes may have to be made if some aspect appears not quite right. First attempts at any creative activity are almost always capable of improvement and the more a presentation is polished in the course of rehearsal, the more it will call for adjustment here and there. But it is tiresome to have to make changes to a structure to which a great deal of effort has already been given and there will be a temptation not to bother. Presenters have to make up their own minds about this and much will depend on their other business commitments, but there is no escaping the reality that without adequate rehearsal the success of the presentation is at risk.

Timing

One thing that cannot be evaded is rehearsal to establish the *time scale*. It is essential to determine how long each section is going to take and this can be done only by running through the presentation at the pace intended. This enables presenters to enter time guides at appropriate places in their notes, so that they can check as they go along whether they are on schedule.

Checking the time may well indicate the need for cuts, additions or adjustments in order to get the balance right. This again should not be seen as a deterrent: it is one of the prime purposes of rehearsal and may be the means of avoiding embarrassment during the actual performance.

Rehearsal of the time scale requires privacy. Those who are afraid of being overheard may prefer to whisper, but it is important to speak every word, without rushing, and make allowances for pauses, repetitions, possible stumbles and the use of visual aids. Account must be taken, too, of the virtual certainty that in private rehearsal a presenter will get through the material faster than before an audience.

Other rehearsal priorities are:

(a) to rehearse the opening and concluding passages, memorising them by repeating them over and over
(b) to become thoroughly familiar with the notes and able to relate to them without hesitation
(c) to go through any visual aids and their place in the presentation.

Priorities apart, the amount of rehearsal depends on the time presenters are prepared, or can afford, to devote to it: the more the better.

Visualisation

There is also a more informal process of which many presenters make use during the period leading up to the performance. They visualise themselves dealing with particularly significant phases of the presentation, such as:

(a) standing up straight, facing the audience, and pausing before delivering their opening words
(b) similarly delivering their closing words, then pausing for a short time before sitting down or moving into question time

(c) any highlight where they may intend to use a particular gesture, or phrase; or
(d) making use of a visual aid.

This can be a valuable means of reassurance, running parallel to, although not, of course, a substitute for, formal rehearsal.

Self-criticism

Rehearsal is concerned principally with the *delivery* of the presentation and, although they are by no means essential, practical aids such as a mirror, tape recorder or video camera can be a great help, if available. (Their use is discussed later in the chapter.) It should be mentioned here that presenters who are obliged to rehearse alone have to be objective and realistically self-critical, a task that calls for self-discipline. It may, for example, be tempting to treat a minor improvement as a major advance and there is, on the other hand, a danger of setting impossibly high standards.

A Candid Colleague

For this reason there is great value in having the assistance from time to time during rehearsal of an independent but understanding observer, who may conveniently be called a "candid colleague". Presenters who can bring themselves to share their problems with another will find that a candid colleague is better than any mechanical aid. The ideal person is one who appreciates what the presenter is trying to achieve, is prepared to give a frank opinion and is capable of standing up to the presenter who, as is occasionally likely, becomes over-defensive. A colleague or friend who meets these specifications is not always easy to find, but the paragon described is worth searching for.

The most candid "colleagues" of all are often one's family. Many regular presenters try out their material at home before risking it on an audience, confident that they will get a frank appraisal motivated by sincere well-wishing.

Self-improvement

It was suggested at the beginning of this chapter that rehearsal should be systematic. This means not only that it should be done in logical steps, but also that it should be controlled. One of the main elements of control is that it should not be allowed to get out of hand and lead to panicky striving for an unattainable perfection. Rehearsal should be thorough, but done with a sense of proportion, which will tell presenters at a certain point that they have gone as far as is reasonably possible.

The most rigorous rehearsal of all is performing before an audience and there can be few presenters who, having completed a presentation, would not wish to make at least some changes. If there is to be a repeat performance they will of course have an opportunity of doing so. In addition, even the most experienced presenters find they learn something new on each occasion and thus acquire increasing experience which they can apply when they rehearse next time.

The best way of improving presentational ability is beyond doubt actually doing it before an audience. The presence of an audience is important, partly because of the resulting feedback and also because experience during practice or rehearsal, even with the help of a candid colleague, is not always a reliable guide to what happens when presenters are on their feet in public.

> It is a common experience to find nothing going right in rehearsal, but the actual performance turns out to be highly successful. This also happens in professional theatrical productions where a bad dress rehearsal is said to be a sure indicator of a sparkling first night. The reason may have something to do with nerves, but it is equally likely that the process of ironing out the bugs, if done properly, can be so uncomfortable that the event itself comes as a relief. It can be compared with the self-imposed pain suffered by an athlete during training.

Practice

Any discussion of self-improvement must, therefore, recognise its limitations. But it is possible at the same time to practise many of the individual aspects of presentation privately in a way that would be impossible before a live audience.

It is, for example, necessary to be away from an audience (except perhaps for colleagues during collective practice sessions) in order to develop some of the basic elements of presentation, such as correct breathing, correct posture, clear articulation and good voice projection, which can be compared with the weight training and muscle exercises performed by an athlete. Shortcomings of this kind can be put right only by practice and more practice. As well as these fundamental accomplishments are the features that add dramatic effect to a presentation: tone of voice, emphasis, pausing, gesture and movement.

A word of reassurance may not be out of place here. There may be some naturally diffident people who fear that, if they acquire some measure of "dramatic" ability as a result of practice, they may appear to an audience to be behaving contrary to their normal personality. This might be a danger if the aim were to produce an exaggerated effect, but this is not the purpose at all. The aim is only to make the delivery of a presentation more interesting and intelligible. Going over the top would diminish rather than enhance the impression conveyed. Practice is valuable not only in developing these attributes but also in ensuring that they are not overdone.

What presenters choose as their medium of practice hardly matters. They can choose passages out of a book or newspaper or make up words of their own, possibly setting them out in the form of notes, which is useful practice for its own sake.

Any initial inhibitions will soon be dispelled as they get into the swing of practising.

Practice is, of course, very close to rehearsal and the two can with advantage run together. It can also be advantageous to use a recent presentation, with the memory of the good and bad things fresh in the mind, as a basis for practice. But practice does not have to be associated with either rehearsal or "post mortem": it has its own value as basic training, which will leave a presenter better equipped and more confident at every stage.

Mechanical Aids

Useful practice is quite possible without human or mechanical assistance, but it has limitations because there is no feedback. Fortunately, mechanical aids are readily available.

Mirror

An obvious piece of equipment is a mirror (if this can be called a mechanical aid), better if it is full length. Its particular usefulness is to give physical feedback, on stance, movement, gesture and facial expression. Watch out objectively for bad habits like fidgeting and over-gesturing. The main drawback of a mirror is that it is necessary to perform and view the performance simultaneously, which tends to undermine concentration.

Tape recorder

For voice alone, a tape recorder is perfect. It is simple to operate and can be played back as often as required. There is no need, however, to stop and try again at every stumble over a word. The better course is to record a reasonably long run, so that when it is played back the overall effect can be judged. If a note is made of the things that need attention, they can then be worked on individually.

Video

Video (camera, recorder and monitor) if available, is the most useful piece of equipment as it enables presenters to see and hear themselves as would an audience. The play back, when a video is used for the first time, can be a surprise, favourable or unfavourable. Objectivity is even more important when using a video, as it is far more of a revelation than tape recorder alone. It is a mistake, on the other hand, to be too self-critical. It is important to be patient and stand back and identify what specifically is going wrong and set out to correct it.

A video camera can be self-operated, if necessary. An object like a chair should be used to adjust the focus and mark out the area within which movement is permissible. It helps to have a short trial run to check the focus before actually starting. An important limitation of self-operation is that the camera has to be in a fixed position and the presenter has to remain within a restricted area. It is therefore not possible, for example, to practise using visual aids. But if there is someone to operate the camera these limitations disappear.

These mechanical aids give feedback, but they cannot offer criticism or encouragement. For this it is necessary to turn to a candid colleague, if the presenter is fortunate enough to have one. As practice is even more tedious for an observer than rehearsal, it is necessary to find someone who has patience, as well as common sense and discrimination, and, for perfection, the ability to operate a video camera.

Many business organisations arrange training courses for their staff in presentational skills. It would be equally useful if they provided audio and video equipment for those who wished to practise. They would be doing an even greater service if they had someone available to coach and encourage and, in effect, fill the role of everyone's in-house candid colleague.

The final thing a self-improver needs is a yardstick and this, fortunately, is readily available in the form of television performers. As suggested earlier, presenters can learn a great deal if they get into the habit of observing professionals and evaluating their good and bad features. Notice how they use their voices; whether they are conscious of and make efforts to help their audiences' understanding; the effectiveness or otherwise of their gestures, especially head and eye. Many are excellent models, as they should be as professional communicators, but most have some weaknesses, which in a few cases are glaring. Television is a different medium from live presentation, but the two have enough in common to enable instructive observations to be made.

Similar observations can, of course, also be made as a member of the audience for a live presentation.

Summary

(a) Rehearsal starts, partly sub-consciously, but uncoordinatedly, as soon as a presentation is contemplated.
(b) To be of real value, rehearsal has to be systematic and there has to be willingness to make changes, if any part of the presentation requires correction.
(c) Rehearsal to determine the time scale and the length of the opening and closing passages is essential, whether or not other aspects are rehearsed.
(d) Apart from formal rehearsal, it is useful for presenters to visualise themselves performing various key elements of the presentation.
(e) The best means of improvement is actually making presentations.
(f) The value of private practice is limited by the absence of an audience, but it is still useful for developing individual skills.
(g) Aids, such as a mirror, tape recorder and video are useful in that there is feedback, but objectivity is necessary.
(h) Candid colleagues, especially if they are able to operate a video

camera (if available), are even more useful because they can also offer criticism and encouragement.

(i) Presenters should get into the habit of identifying good and bad points in other presenters (for example, on television) and applying the lessons to themselves.

Chapter 10
Conclusion

The ability to make a successful presentation is within the compass of virtually all business people, even those who have hitherto convinced themselves that they lack the necessary natural gifts. The aim of this guide has been to try to remove the mystique which seems to surround the subject. Its method has been to examine the principles of effective presentation, to identify what is good and what is bad practice and to suggest a systematic drill by means of which any presentation can be approached with reasonable confidence in its success.

The guide does not offer a panacea: to become a successful presenter requires application and willingness to continue the learning process in the course of gaining experience. And even for one who has acquired reasonable mastery, success in a presentation can be measured in direct proportion to the thoroughness of preparation. There are no short cuts, but the prize is surely worthwhile: there can be few doubts about this among the countless number of business people who have been on the receiving end of ineffective presentations in the course of their work.

Each chapter has used the three step formula recommended for presentations:

(a) introduction,
(b) development and
(c) summing up,

and it is appropriate that the guide should end with an overall summary of its contents.

Summary of the Guide

(a) Successful presentation is an important skill in an age when business people rightly feel entitled to be the recipients of clear communications about matters that concern them.

(b) The first hurdle to overcome is nerves, which result from a wish to perform creditably in the unpredictable circumstances of making a presentation to an audience. Nerves should not be thought of as a deterrent but as something normal and healthy, which keeps presenters on their toes and complacency at bay.

(c) Knowledge of the facts is an essential basis for a successful presentation.

(d) Preparation should be as thorough as possible, starting with a clear definition of purpose. Presenters should remember that no audience can assimilate more than a limited amount in one go and, keeping this in mind, construct a logical, interesting text, using simple, familiar and unambiguous language.

(e) The material should be divided into the categories: essential, non-essential and anecdotal. Anecdotes provide a leavening for the dry facts.

(f) A reliable method of arranging the text is the three step formula: introduction, development and summing up.

(g) Simple and comprehensible visual aids should be used, without overdoing them, for emphasis or illustration.

(h) A script read out word for word, unless expertly delivered, lacks spontaneity and sparkle. It is better to use notes, neatly and logically set out.

(i) Take trouble over the administrative arrangements.

(j) The audience are all important. A presentation which fails to get a positive response from the audience has failed in its purpose.

(k) Time is precious in business and presenters who take too long are in danger of losing their audience, however competent their performance in other respects. Keep a check on time.

(l) Presenters can achieve an intelligible and interesting delivery through various methods of paragraphing, signposting, emphasis, and changing the pace and pitch of the voice.

(m) Amiability is an asset in a presenter. Topical one liners are a more reliable form of humour than jokes. If an attempt at humour misfires, move on quickly.

(n) Audibility is vital and is assisted by correct posture, breathing, articulation and projection.
(o) A presentation can be enlivened with relevant, confident and discreet gestures, those of the head and eyes being particularly effective. Any movement should be purposeful.
(p) Fidgeting and distracting mannerisms should be avoided.
(q) Allow plenty of time for questions, which should be answered briefly and honestly.
(r) Audiences often welcome a summary of the presentation in the form of a simple, attractive handout.
(s) Rehearsal, particularly of the time scale and the opening and closing passages, is always advantageous,
(t) The best way to improve is actually to make presentations, but practising the component skills is also useful.

Index